## PRAISE FOR
# THE EMOTIONAL LIVES OF TEENAGERS

■ ■ ■ ■ ■

"How are we supposed to get our kids through these daunting years? There are countless books on the subject, but *The Emotional Lives of Teenagers* is the nuanced, empathetic one I wish I'd had when I was in the trenches."

—*The New York Times*

"*The Emotional Lives of Teenagers* does a very simple and very difficult thing. It helps me feel ready for the joy, and the storm, to come."

—*Slate*

"Filled with relatable situations, examples, and suggestions for constructive conversations, this book will be welcomed by parents and anyone who works with adolescents. Parents looking for timely advice and reassurance will find it here in clear layman's language."

—*Booklist*

"A calm, wise, and empathetic guide to a difficult period for both adolescents and parents."

—*Kirkus Reviews*

"Damour's down-to-earth tone gives this the feel of a conversation with a friend, while the psychology offers valuable perspective into the scientific underpinnings of adolescence. Parents of teens will want to check this out."

—*Publishers Weekly*

"*The Emotional Lives of Teenagers* is written as clearly, usefully, and warmly as anything I've read about the psychology of adolescence. Lisa Damour explains why intense feelings—including negative ones—are a key part of teenage development, and how we can help young people understand and *embrace* the full spectrum of human emotion. I give it my highest recommendation!"

—ANGELA DUCKWORTH, author of *Grit* and co-founder of Character Lab

"Lisa Damour applies her decades of clinical experience to one of the most essential questions of our time: How can adults best support adolescent mental health? She hands parents, teachers, coaches, and mentors the playbook they need to help teenagers feel heard, healthy, and whole."

—JEWEL, singer-songwriter and mental health advocate

"This book offers a crucial reframing that helps parents understand teens, their emotions, and their behavior. I couldn't love it more. Damour gifts us with knowledge, words, and practical advice to reach our teenagers so that we can be the parents they need us to be as they become fully themselves."

—TINA PAYNE BRYSON, co-author of *The Whole-Brain Child*

"Dr. Damour dispels harmful but pervasive myths about teen mental health. If, like most parents, you find yourself alienated or confused by your teen's unpredictable feelings, add this book to the top of your reading pile immediately."

—MICHELLE ICARD, author of *Fourteen Talks by Age Fourteen*

"I can't recommend this book enough. Damour gives parents practical, actionable, research-backed advice to ensure their children develop the emotional skills they need to thrive."

—MARC BRACKETT, director, Yale Center for Emotional Intelligence and author of *Permission to Feel*

## By Lisa Damour

The Emotional Lives of Teenagers
Under Pressure
Untangled

# THE EMOTIONAL
# LIVES OF TEENAGERS

# RAISING CONNECTED, CAPABLE, AND COMPASSIONATE ADOLESCENTS

BALLANTINE BOOKS
NEW YORK

# THE EMOTIONAL
# LIVES OF TEENAGERS

LISA DAMOUR, Ph.D.

2024 Ballantine Books Trade Paperback Edition

Published in the United States by Ballantine Books, an imprint of Random House, a division of Penguin Random House LLC, New York.

BALLANTINE BOOKS & colophon are registered trademarks of Penguin Random House LLC.

Originally published in hardcover in the United States by Ballantine Books, an imprint of Random House, a division of Penguin Random House LLC, in 2023.

Grateful acknowledgment is made to Taylor & Francis Ltd. for permission to reprint an excerpt from pg. 275 of Anna Freud (1958) "Adolescence," *The Psychoanalytic Study of the Child* 13:1, 255-278, https://doi.org/10.1080/00797308.1958.11823182. Reprinted by permission of the publisher, Taylor & Francis Ltd, http://www.tandfonline.com.

LIBRARY OF CONGRESS CATALOGING-IN-PUBLICATION DATA
Names: Damour, Lisa, author.
Title: The emotional lives of teenagers: raising connected, capable, and compassionate adolescents / Lisa Damour, Ph.D.
Description: First edition. | New York: Ballantine Group, 2023.
Identifiers: LCCN 2022032622 (print) | LCCN 2022032623 (ebook) | ISBN 9780593500033 (trade paperback) | ISBN 9780593500026 (ebook)
Subjects: LCSH: Emotions in adolescence. | Teenagers—Social conditions. | Parent and teenager.
Classification: LCC BF724.3.E5 D36 2023 (print) | LCC BF724.3.E5 (ebook) | DDC 155.5/124—dc23/eng/20220729
LC record available at https://lccn.loc.gov/2022032622
LC ebook record available at https://lccn.loc.gov/2022032623

Printed in the United States of America on acid-free paper

randomhousebooks.com

2 4 6 8 9 7 5 3 1

*Book design by Simon M. Sullivan*

Images on pages iv and v: Franciso; highwaystarz; a4stockphotos; bestforlater91; iordani; Valua Vitaly; DisoberyArt; Вячеслав Чичаев; auremar; FABIAN PONCE GARCIA; Aleksandr; themorningglory; rimmdream/all via stock.adobe.com

To D, my much better half.

I take it that it is normal for an adolescent to behave for a considerable length of time in an inconsistent and unpredictable manner; to fight his impulses and to accept them . . . to love his parents and to hate them . . . to revolt against them and be dependent on them . . . to be more idealistic, artistic, generous, and unselfish than he will ever be again, but also the opposite: self-centered, egoistic, calculating. Such fluctuations between extreme opposites would be deemed highly abnormal at any other time of life. At this time they signify no more than that an adult structure of personality takes a long time to emerge.

—ANNA FREUD (1958)


It is a deep comfort to children to discover that their feelings are a normal part of the human experience.

—HAIM GINOTT (1965)

# Contents

■ ■ ■ ■ ■

CHAPTER FIVE ■ **Managing Emotions, Part Two:**
**Helping Teens Regain Emotional Control**             **145**

**Conclusion**                                         **183**

# Introduction

■ ■ ■ ■ ■

In June 2021, I got a call from a friend I've known since middle school. We caught up briefly about what had happened in our lives and our families since we last talked, and then she said, "Actually, there's a reason I'm calling ... I'm really worried about Will. Can I run something by you?"

"Of course," I replied, recalling that her son Will, like my own older daughter, was about to be a high school senior.

"A couple of weeks ago, we learned that my husband's company is transferring us to Seattle. We're moving at the end of the summer and Will is a mess about it. He loves his friends and his school here in Denver and he can't believe that we're uprooting him right before his senior year. He's been incredibly cranky, and in the last couple of days he's even gotten tearful about it. I don't know what to say to make things better, and I'm getting worried that he might be depressed."

"Is his mood down all the time, or does it rise and fall in waves?" I asked.

"It rises and falls. When he's not thinking about moving, he actually seems to be okay. He has a job that he likes, and he's plenty happy when he's hanging out with his friends. But when the topic of the move comes up, he gets so, so sad. I don't know what to do, and can't tell if I should be worried."

"Listen," I said, "I don't think he's depressed. But let's stay in close touch, because I'll want to know if his mood stops going up and down and instead he starts spending most of his time feeling cranky, numb, or blue. From what you're telling me, it sounds as if he's unhappy specifically about the move—that he's feeling sad and angry about it."

"Absolutely," said my friend.

"But I don't consider these grounds for concern. Actually, I think those feelings are evidence of his *good* mental health."

"Really? How?"

"Well, being upset about moving right before senior year— especially when he's happy in Denver—is an entirely appropriate response. I'd actually be more worried about Will if it didn't bother him at all."

"That makes sense, I guess," my friend said, "but how am I supposed to help him through it?"

"There are two things you can do. First, reassure Will that he's having the right reaction. Just as it's hard for you to see him so upset, having such painful emotions is probably uncomfortable for him, too. You can help to put his mind at ease by letting him know that what he's feeling makes sense. Second, try to get comfortable with the idea that he's probably going to continue to be unhappy about the situation, at least until he gets settled in the fall. Rather than working to prevent or chase away his discomfort, focus your attention on helping him find ways to manage the distress he's feeling."

For teenagers, powerful emotions are a feature, not a bug. This has always been true, but these days it seems to be less widely understood. The past decade especially has been marked by a dramatic shift in how we talk and think about feelings in general and, in particular, about the intense emotions that characterize adolescence.

To put it bluntly, somewhere along the way we became afraid of being unhappy.

When I received my first license to practice clinically as a psychologist nearly thirty years ago, I had been steeped in a training program that embraced the full range of emotion—a spectrum of feelings from the most pleasant to the least—as an expectable and *essential* aspect of the human experience.

My training taught me to regard adolescents' emotional landscapes with an observant, unafraid eye. I have always understood psychotherapy to be a joint enterprise in which I guide the teenagers in my care to share my curiosity about their inner lives. We work from the unspoken assumption that every one of their emotions makes sense, that their difficult feelings—anger, frustration, sadness, worry, and the rest—happen for a reason, even when the reasons for them are unclear. Though of course I'm there to help them feel better, the aim of our work is less about comfort and more about insight. When teenagers *understand* what they are feeling and why, they suddenly have choices that were not available to them before.

To me, this is axiomatic. I have never doubted or questioned the value of welcoming even the most distressing or disturbing emotions into the light of my office. But as I've worked away in my practice, watching the process of young people discovering, understanding, and accepting their emotions and receiving much-needed and deserved relief, I have sensed the culture around me changing. Twenty years ago, I still felt myself to be part of a broader society that accepted, albeit begrudgingly, that painful feelings are a natural part of life. Today, I am trying to figure out how uncomfortable feelings came to be seen as psychological states that ought to be prevented or, failing that, banished as quickly as possible.

What changed? How did essential aspects of the human condition become unacceptable?

How exactly this happened I can't know for sure, but I have some ideas. Since the time of my training, three trends have emerged that may help explain the shift in how we view psychological distress: the proliferation of effective psychiatric medications, the rise of the wellness industry, and the climbing numbers of young people who suffer from mental health disorders. Let's weigh these one by one.

Antidepressant medications have been available since the 1950s, but they were not widely prescribed until the late 1980s, when Prozac hit the market. Let me say right here that Prozac and the many other psychiatric medications that have been developed in recent years dramatically improve, and sometimes save, lives. Before physicians began to prescribe Prozac in 1987, they worked with so-called "first generation" antidepressant medications. While these drugs were often effective, they caused miserable side effects and could be lethal in overdose (a tragic problem when caring for suicidal patients). Then along came Prozac and, soon after, an entire "second generation" of medications that lifted depression and had minimal side effects. Suddenly, prescription drugs became a low-risk option for mood improvement.

It's no wonder these drugs took off. In 1987 only 37 percent of those being treated for depression received an antidepressant. By 2015 that number had risen to 81 percent. During that same period, the number of people receiving psychotherapy for depression dropped by 20 percent. What drove these two trends? First, it's likely that antidepressant medication provided some individuals with enough relief that psychotherapy no longer felt necessary. Second, it's also true that insurance companies are far more willing to pay for pills than for sometimes costly talk therapy.

To these explanations, I'll also add a third possibility: The proliferation of safe and effective medications to treat depression—and also to reduce anxiety, improve sleep, and focus attention—has altered our cultural stance toward emotional discomfort. Instead of regarding psychological unease as something to be explored and understood, we have increasingly come to view emotional pain as something that can be deterred or contained with chemical interventions. Numbers don't lie: Since the early 2000s, antidepressants have been on par with blood pressure and cholesterol medications as the most prescribed drugs in adult outpatient visits.

To be clear: There is no question that psychiatric drugs ease human suffering. Further, no conscientious clinician prescribes these medications with the promise that they will solve life's problems or make people happy, because they don't. That said, I can't help but wonder whether the widespread use of mood-altering drugs has stoked the belief that somehow we and our children might and should be spared the reality that being human comes with feeling emotional pain.

I do not, however, think that the rapid proliferation of psychiatric medications can, alone, account for the fact that we've become so uneasy with psychological discomfort. So let's turn our attention to a second factor: the wellness industry.

Wellness is hardly new. Yoga, mindfulness, aromatherapy, and a host of nonmedical practices and products associated with psychological health have been around for millennia. What *is* new? The pervasive and aggressive marketing of wellness goods and services. In 2010, a business article in *The New York Times* referred to wellness as an "emerging" industry. Since then, the commercial wellness market has done nothing short of explode. Now an economic juggernaut, the mental wellness industry alone accounts for $131 billion of the global wellness economy. To put this number in perspective, the mental wellness industry now outmatches the $100 billion global entertainment industry.

Of course this isn't bad news. Studies consistently demonstrate that meditation, mindfulness, and yoga practices can ease psychological discomfort and improve mental well-being. Botanical-infused lotions, aromatic candles, weighted blankets, and other products that delight or soothe the senses can, without question, bring about short-term feelings of peace and relief.

All the same, it seems to be the case that massive economic incentives are now driving the wellness industry to make promises it cannot keep. Advertisements for self-care products often declare or imply that the product for sale (be it a mindfulness app, a scented oil, or a fruity tea) will both grant feelings of ease *and* ward off unwanted emotions. This might sound great in theory, but common sense tells us that's not how life actually works. Enjoying your yoga class won't keep the school principal from calling with news that your kid hit a classmate on the playground. Getting your family to commit to a regular mindfulness practice won't keep a global pandemic from delivering years of misery to your door. Wellness products or practices *can* temporarily lift our spirits or help us regain a passing sense of equilibrium. They *cannot* shield us, or our teenagers, from emotional distress.

We know this and we don't. It's incredibly tempting to believe in the possibility of attaining and preserving a state of psychological ease, especially when ubiquitous wellness ads suggest that an unruffled Zen state can be achieved. Or at least purchased.

While the expectations set by the wellness industry border on the ridiculous, their impact is no joke. I now care for teenagers in my practice who feel as if they are "failing at wellness." They've taken to heart the dangerous message, often promoted through social media marketing, that committing to self-care—and the goods and services that come with it—will keep them from feeling stressed or anxious. Then semester exams hit. When this happens, our teens naturally experience the tension and nerves that *always* come with taking big tests. But now they feel worse than we ever did at the end of the term, as wall-to-wall advertising suggests that their discomfort was somehow preventable. Our already stressed teenagers now feel bad about feeling bad.

Further, the rise of the wellness industry seems to have shifted how our culture defines psychological health. In roughly the last ten years—the same span in which mental wellness became a multi-billion-dollar industry—psychological health has become equated with feeling good. Of course, it's great to feel good (or calm, or relaxed), but the reality is that pleasant psychological states come and go as we move through our day. No matter what we do, there's no guarantee that any one of us can sustain an extended period of untroubled ease.

This now widespread message that mental health means feeling *good* has led many parents and teenagers to its logical corollary, that feeling *bad* is grounds for serious concern. I worry that the wellness movement has left parents and their teens unduly frightened of garden variety adversity. Now, far more than in years past, I find myself needing to reassure adolescents and their folks that a rough day or a rough week is unlikely to be a sign that "something is really wrong."

Which brings us to the third factor that might explain how we find ourselves at a time when teenagers and their parents feel more uneasy than ever about emotional distress: Adolescents, as a group, actually do feel worse than they used to.

Some of this has to do with the fact that our teenagers face the unsettling prospect of a future marked by ongoing environmental, social, and political turmoil. A 2018 survey conducted by the American Psychological Association found that, compared to adults overall, people between the ages of fifteen and twenty-one express higher levels of concern about the direction in which the nation is headed, the prevalence of mass shootings, and climate change.

Among teenagers, more serious mental health concerns have also been on the rise. From 2009 to 2019, the percentage of high school students who reported feeling persistently sad or hopeless jumped from 26 percent to 37 percent; the percentage who told survey takers they had made a suicide plan grew from an already startling 11 percent to an even more alarming 16 percent. In about the same time frame, the percentage of high school students reporting significant levels of anxiety rose from 34 percent to 44 percent. These grim statistics, as you likely noticed, reflect how teenagers were feeling *before* a pandemic crashed into their formative years.

While the pandemic was horrible for everyone, teenagers faced unique challenges, precisely because COVID-19 derailed the central developmental tasks of adolescence, namely, spending time with peers and becoming increasingly independent. Global studies found that symptoms of depression and anxiety among teens doubled during the pandemic and that many started to have difficulty sleeping, withdrew from their families, or became aggressive. Studies conducted by emergency medicine departments in early 2021 found that visits for suspected suicide attempts increased by 51 percent among teenage girls and 4 percent among teenage boys, compared to visits in early 2019. Experts are not entirely sure what accounts for the huge gender disparity in increased attempts but suspect that girls may have felt the social isolation of the pandemic more acutely than boys did.

The situation was even worse for teenagers belonging to racial and ethnic groups that have long been marginalized and discriminated against. Compared to white teenagers, Black, Asian American, and multiracial adolescents experienced higher levels of pandemic-related psychological distress. The pandemic was of course also overlaid with a great number of other national crises that affected our teenagers: intense political polarization, rising violence, and a painful and necessary reckoning with the killing of Black Americans by police.

It's no wonder that so many of today's parents worry about their teens' mental health. Being a teenager has always been hard; coming of age during a time of widespread disruption makes the work of being a teenager—or raising one—that much more difficult. With crisis, though, often comes opportunity, and in fact I believe there has never been a better time to get serious about how we support teenagers and their emotional lives.

In the decade prior to the pandemic, I wrote two books that focused on the challenges faced specifically by girls and young women. Under COVID-19, my attention shifted unsurprisingly to the pressing emotional needs of all teenagers, irrespective of gender. This was an easy transition, as in more than three decades as a clinician I've cared for many boys and young men. Further, my *New York Times* articles about adolescence and my *Ask Lisa* podcast have never been gender-specific. Throughout this book, examples from my clinical work with both boys and girls will illustrate key ideas. For these, all identifying details have been altered, and in a few cases I've presented composites in order to maintain the confidentiality of the young people who have been in my care.

You are reading this book because you care about adolescents. You want to help teens navigate a challenging phase of life during a challenging time in history. You want to raise them to have rich and rewarding emotional lives, to be caring and connected in their relationships, to remain steady and capable in good times and bad, and to develop true emotional strength.

This book will help you do just that. In the first chapter we'll dispel widely held and misleading myths about how feelings operate and instead ground our exploration of the emotional lives of teenagers in psychological science. Chapter 2 will address how traditional gender roles shape the experience and expression of adolescent emotion and unpack what new understandings of gender mean for teenagers and their parents. In chapter 3 we'll look at what is unique about emotions during adolescence and how they put a new spin on everyday life for teens and their families. Chapters 4 and 5 draw on clinical research and theory to offer parents concrete, practical guidance on helping teenagers develop independent emotional lives by finding healthy ways to express their emotions and, when needed, bring them under control.

Perhaps most important, this book will ditch the dangerous view that adolescents are mentally healthy only when they can sustain a sense of feeling good. In its place, we'll get to know a truly useful and psychologically accurate definition of emotional health: having the right feelings at the right time and being able to manage those feelings effectively.

Let's not wait another moment to better understand and support the teenagers we love.

# THE EMOTIONAL
# LIVES OF TEENAGERS

## CHAPTER ONE

# Adolescent Emotion 101:
# Getting Past Three Big Myths

"Dr. D," the text read, "can I come c you sometime this week? Tom." I didn't recognize the phone number it was coming from and had no one named Tom on my weekly practice schedule. As I stared curiously at my phone, three dots materialized, followed by a message that seemed to come from a mind reader: "It's me Tommy—I got your number from my mom."

Tommy! Of course. I immediately remembered a sweet nine-year-old I'd first laid eyes on in my waiting room years earlier. When we met, he was standing anxiously next to his mother as she sat with one hand resting calmly in her lap and the other gently stroking her son's back. Any progress she'd made in trying to ease his nerves evaporated when I opened the waiting room door. Tommy took me in with wide-eyed dread. His dark hair stood up on one side—bedhead that had impressively survived an entire school day—seeming to underscore his overall sense of alarm. On the phone, Tommy's mother had explained that he was having nighttime fears that were keeping him and the rest of the family up late. At my office, Tommy and his mom followed me to my consulting room, and there we slowly began what would grow into a long and fruitful working relationship.

Tommy was born tense. As a baby he startled easily and went

on to have enormous difficulty separating from his parents when it was time to go to preschool. His worries morphed over the years into nighttime fears, which thankfully yielded to my efforts to be helpful and his parents' steady support. After those fears were resolved, nearly two years passed before I heard from his folks again. In the summer after seventh grade, Tommy bravely tried going to sleepaway camp but within two days was begging to come home. I had a few calls with Tommy at camp and several with his parents, and I also consulted by phone with the camp director. Together, we decided to pull the plug, with the hope of trying camp again the next year. Tommy met with me throughout that summer, both to address the anxiety that brought him home and to process his feelings of frustration and humiliation around being unable to stay.

Remembering all of this as I looked at my phone, I realized that nearly four years had gone by since I'd last heard from Tommy—now Tom—or his parents, which would make him a high school senior. We set up a time to meet and I prepared myself for the likelihood that I'd hardly recognize the person in my waiting room. Sure enough, Tom was now tall and broad-shouldered. He was wearing long, loose shorts that were poorly suited to the chilly late-October temperatures in the suburbs of Greater Cleveland. At once awkward and friendly, he greeted me with a deep voice that I didn't recognize.

After we settled into my office and caught up briefly, he turned to the reason for his text.

"I'm working on my college applications and don't want to apply too far from home. I'm okay with this, and my parents are too, but my college counselor is kinda making a thing of it."

Tom was at the top of his class, thanks, no doubt, to the fact that his anxious temperament also made him a highly conscientious student. He was a sought-after cross-country runner and had also developed into an accomplished oboist. Despite the many ways he had matured, Tom explained that although he had hoped to attend a five-week intensive music program in Michigan the previous summer, he could not bring himself to go. Based on that experience, he decided to apply only to colleges within a three-hour drive of home.

Northeast Ohio has no shortage of excellent colleges and universities, but the college counselor at Tom's school still felt that Tom was limiting his opportunities. I wasn't sure what to think. From the gray couch in my office, Tom shared his reasoning with me. If he started to feel nervous or unsure when he was away at college, Tom wanted to be able to come home for a night or two without its being a big deal. He was sending applications to seven very fine area schools—he would certainly have excellent options when the admissions decisions came in. And he wasn't applying to any college within thirty minutes of his house, because he really did want to feel that he'd gone *away* to school.

"I still get super anxious," Tom said. "It's better than it was, for sure, but I've never liked being away from my family. I'm just trying to come up with a solution that doesn't leave me feeling like my anxiety could mess up my freshman year. When I explained this to my college counselor, he said: 'Tom, your worries are clouding your thinking.'"

Though I knew where the counselor was coming from, I didn't share his perspective. To me, it seemed to be grounded in an unhelpful but well-worn myth: that our feelings undermine our judgment.

## Myth #1: Emotion Is the Enemy of Reason

Emotions and reason were cast as competitors long before Mr. Spock, with his reasoning unsullied by emotion, was showcased as *Star Trek*'s model thinker. Indeed, the opposition between our thoughts and our feelings has seemed so apparent that philosophers have commented on it for ages. Plato imagined reason as a charioteer working to keep the horses of human emotion under control; René Descartes, a champion of rationality, idealized those who "are entirely masters of their passions," while David Hume, flipping Descartes's script, argued that "Reason is, and ought only to be the slave of the passions."

So how should we think about the place of emotions in decision making? Plato, Descartes, Hume—who has it right?

Probably my friend Terry does. She's a fellow clinical psychologist who once shared a terrifically useful metaphor with me. According to Terry, when it comes to decision making, we ought to view our emotions as occupying one seat on our personal board of directors. Other spots on the board might be held by ethical considerations, our personal ambitions, our obligations to others, financial or logistical constraints, and so on. Ideally, these board members will work together to help us make careful, informed choices about how we conduct our lives. In this metaphor, emotions have a vote, though it's rarely a deciding one. And they definitely don't chair the board.

Terry's take finds support in psychological research. Studies show that, under the right conditions, our feelings can in fact improve the quality of our decision making. To examine how emotions influence reasoning, the psychologist Isabelle Blanchette asked British war veterans to solve logic problems on three different topics. One subset of the topics was combat-related (e.g., "Some chemical weapons are used in wars. All things used in wars are dangerous. Therefore, some chemical weapons are dangerous"); a second was emotionally loaded but *not* combat-related (e.g., "Some cancers are hereditary . . ."); and the third was emotionally neutral (e.g., "Some teas are natural substances . . ."). The fascinating result? The veterans reasoned most soundly when given logic problems related to combat. Their emotional investment in war-related topics seemed to bolster their ability to make accurate deductions.

Blanchette's war veteran study included a further wrinkle that sheds light on the interaction between emotion and logical thinking. In her study, half of the veterans suffered from post-traumatic stress disorder (PTSD), which is characterized by painful, disruptive thoughts and feelings related to a past traumatic event. Blanchette found that veterans who suffered from PTSD underperformed on every category of the logic problems as compared to those who did not. Having a degree of personal investment in a topic can improve reasoning, but *too much* emotion creates a cognitive drag that interferes with our thinking.

So where does all of this leave Tom? In my opinion, his feelings were serving as a valuable contributor to his internal board meeting. He knew from experience that he had a hard time leaving home, but his emotions were not so powerful that they were crowding out other thoughtful considerations. Tom wanted to be near his family, but not *too* near, in case things went well and he felt ready to be independent. He cared about school and wanted to have choices about where he went to college. Thanks to his good fortune in living in a region rich with higher educational options, Tom could check all of these boxes without having to look far from home.

"It seems to me," I said, "that you've really thought this through. Given that this will be the first time that you're truly going away, it makes sense that you'd want to do so with a safety net. Even if you never use it, you'll feel better knowing it's there."

"That's how *I* feel," replied Tom, "but what am I supposed to say to my college counselor?"

"I think you can let him know that you appreciate his concern, and that while it can seem like your worries are calling the shots, they're actually just one of many factors guiding your decision making."

We went on to talk about what really mattered to Tom as he thought about his transition to college. He wanted to be able to look forward to heading off to school and to feel that he could succeed once he got there. Input from his emotions helped him arrive at a solution that met both these goals. Tom's anxiety was serving as a wise, measured member of his personal decision-making board.

### Helping Teenagers Learn to Trust Their Gut

First and foremost, we want our teenagers to regard their feelings in this important way: as data. Whether painful or pleasant, emotions are fundamentally informational. They bubble up as we move through our days, delivering meaningful feedback. Our emotions give us status reports on our lives and can help guide decision making. Noticing that you feel upbeat and energized after a lunch with a particular friend might inspire you to spend more time with that person. Realizing that you're dreading an upcoming office party might get you thinking about whether it's really worth attending this year. Rather than viewing our emotions as disruptive, we're usually better off if we treat them as a constant stream of messengers arriving with updates on how things are going.

Teenagers don't always see their feelings this way. Adolescents are often torn between the signals they're receiving from the outside world and those arising from within. They can doubt the validity of their own emotions, especially when their feelings don't line up with what their peers seem to feel. For instance, a teenager who becomes uncomfortable about something her friends seem okay with doing—such as badmouthing a classmate, experimenting with marijuana, or cutting class—will sometimes go round and round trying to figure out who's got it right.

She'll wonder if her friends are in the wrong, or if she's being uptight.

An adolescent will sometimes bring up a dilemma like this at home in a way that adults can find confounding. Adopting a nonchalant air, your daughter might offhandedly mention that "Some girls in my grade skipped physics to go out to lunch." It can be shocking to have a teenager share concerning news in such a casual tone. Cutting class is a big deal, we may be thinking, and it's even worse that our own kid seems okay with it. Before we launch into a lecture, it's worth entertaining the possibility that our teen may not know how to feel about the situation herself and is feigning indifference as a way to get a read on how *we* feel about it. Looked at this way, a stern lecture might not be the worst option. Our teenager will at least know that she's not the only one who thinks her peers are over the line, even if she might not give us the satisfaction of letting us know that she sees it the same way we do.

Still, asking a genuine question would be a better bet. A gentle "Hmm . . . how do you feel about that?" lets our teen know that we're not comfortable with what her classmates did, and that we suspect she may feel the same way. Now we're pointed in a promising direction. When we show that we are curious about our adolescents' feelings—especially around the topics they bring up—we invite them to treat their emotions as informative and trustworthy. Teenagers almost always rise to meet us when we treat them as the deeply insightful souls that they are. Don't be surprised if the teen who was casually sharing provocative news only moments ago abruptly switches gears to respond thoughtfully by saying, "I guess it makes me feel worried about them," or something along those lines.

What if, however, you try this approach and find that your teen is in *no mood* for an earnest conversation? Indeed, asking for thoughts on a peer's dicey behavior could easily be met with an annoyed (if not flat-out hostile) response. Even if you feel that you hit a brick wall, don't despair. As far as I'm concerned, the conversation was already a success. When teens bring up their peers' antics at home, they're usually looking for a reality check. Raising our proverbial eyebrows—even if teens get mad at us for doing so—gives them just that.

Above all, we want to look for opportunities to drive home the key point that our emotions help us navigate our lives. Ignoring our feelings means flying blind. Any time we hear our teenagers questioning feelings that make abundant sense given the situation, we should be quick to lay on the reassurance. "You have a good gut," we might say. "Pay attention to what it's telling you, because it will almost always keep you on the right track."

Tom, it turned out, was wise to listen to himself. He was accepted at several colleges and decided to attend a small liberal arts school about an hour from home. Though in the summer before his first year he was excited about going off to college, his first semester was rocky. He got along well with his roommate, but being away from home was unsettling and made it very hard for him to sleep at night. As Tom's fatigue increased, his anxiety rose right along with it, setting off a vicious cycle that further undermined his sleep. We picked up our work again, now through virtual sessions at times when Tom had his dorm room to himself. It quickly became clear that he needed to come home for a few days to catch up on sleep, and also to meet with one of my psychiatric colleagues for a consultation about medication.

For much of October and early November, Tom returned home on Thursdays after his last class of the week and then went back to school on Sunday afternoons, feeling restored by spending time with his folks, visiting with his longtime music teacher, and getting to sleep in his own bed. He was intensely frustrated that he was missing out on the college's weekend activities, but he started to enjoy the time he did spend at school much more for knowing he was only ever a few days away from being able to recharge at home.

With the help of our regular therapy sessions, medication that took the edge off his anxiety, an understanding roommate, and supportive parents, Tom started to stay at school for longer stretches. Two weeks into the second semester, his music teacher encouraged him to audition for the college orchestra. Tom was surprised—and honored—to be named principal oboist. From there, his situation improved rapidly. Rehearsals and concerts quickly filled Tom's schedule, making it impossible for him to come home. Thankfully, he now rarely wanted or needed to. By April, he was signing a fall lease for an off-campus apartment that he would share with two good friends he had met in the orchestra.

Tom reached out to me only once more that year, when his grandmother died unexpectedly. We met twice to help him process his grief and shock. After that, I heard nothing until late fall of Tom's sophomore year, when I ran into his mother at the grocery store. She gave me the full report on how he was doing. "He couldn't be happier." She beamed. "We go to some of his performances, but he only comes home during school breaks, and sometimes not even then. Honestly, at this point, he might as well be in school in California."

## A Caveat: Teen Judgment Can Be Context-Dependent

It was clear in retrospect that Tom was wise to let his worries have a say in his college plans. His story is an excellent example of how emotions can improve the quality of an adolescent's decision making. But this isn't always the case. There are certainly times when teenagers can find themselves in situations where emotions *do* get in the way of their better judgment.

Teenagers, far more than children or adults, can be prone to making bad decisions when doing exciting things with their friends. I doubt you're surprised to hear this. As a former teenager yourself, you can probably remember a time when you, or some kids you knew, did some astonishingly dumb stuff because other kids were doing it too.

For me, it was "skitching." I grew up in Colorado and was a teenager in the 1980s when Denver was still a small town. After a heavy snowfall, the empty late-night streets would be covered in a packed, slippery layer of snow. In these conditions, we would go out well after dark, grab onto the back bumper of a friend's car two or three at a time, yell for our driving friend to hit the gas, then enjoy being pulled while in a squat position, our boots like skis, at ever increasing speeds. Eventually our grip would give out and we'd be left in a heap on the snowy road, at which point the driver would circle around and we'd begin again. Between turns on the bumper, we'd sit facing backward in the open trunk chatting with the active skitchers. Recalling this now in my midfifties, I can't believe what we did, and as the mother of two teenagers, I'd be on the ceiling if one of my own daughters did anything like this. But I also remember how those late-night skitching sessions felt. They were so much fun that I didn't even think about danger. My good friends were skitching, so I wanted to skitch, too.

At the risk of sounding defensive, I feel the need to note that, as teenagers go, I was pretty level-headed overall. My skitching was not part of a broader pattern of reckless or impulsive behavior. Had my parents known what we were up to and asked me to detail the potential hazards of skitching, I could, even then, have generated a long list of its actual dangers. But when we were out in the snow, I wasn't weighing what could go wrong. I was having fun with my friends.

Psychologists have discovered that when thinking about risky behaviors, teenagers are almost quite literally of two minds. There's the "assessing-danger-in-the-cold-light-of-day" mind, and there's the "I'm-with-my-friends-and-we're-having-fun" mind. These two different mindsets are referred to respectively as *cold* and *hot cognition,* and the one that's in charge depends on where teenagers are and what's happening around them.

Under cold cognition conditions, such as when your teen is standing in your kitchen on a Saturday afternoon describing his plans for the night, teenagers have a great capacity for sound and prudent reasoning. But in the heat of a social moment, hot cognition kicks in and they think less carefully about risk. Your teenager may be telling you the God's honest truth when he says he has no intention of drinking, smoking, or doing anything else that might be dangerous that evening. But when he gets to a party and discovers that all of his friends are drinking, there's a decent chance that hot cognition will take over and he'll join in.

What are adults supposed to do with the news that all teens lead a terrifying mental double life? First, they can take comfort in knowing that many states have crafted laws to account for the fact that teens take more risks when they are with their peers. Graduated driver's licenses restrict the number of adolescent passengers in a new driver's car because the likelihood that a sixteen- or seventeen-year-old will have an accident rises with every additional agemate on board. Why? Because the teenage brain is unusually sensitive to both the pleasures of engaging in new or exciting experiences, such as driving fast or recklessly, and also the social rewards of feeling accepted by one's peers. Combine these two factors, as happens with a carful of friends, and driving can quickly become dangerous. Awareness among legislators of the power of hot cognition has resulted in licensing laws that have dramatically reduced automobile accidents among teenagers.

Second, knowing that our teens can spontaneously shift from cold to hot reasoning, we should think, *in advance,* about how they'll make decisions when they find themselves in the kind of heady social situation that is likely to flip the switch. We should capitalize on times when teenagers have cold, analytic reasoning on their side, such as the afternoon kitchen conversation, to ask them how they'll handle themselves when hot, impulse-boosting conditions kick in.

When your teenager reassures you that he won't be drinking at the party he's planning to attend, try saying, "So glad to hear it! Now, what will you do if you get there and all your friends *are* drinking? How will you stick to your plan?" Clever teens use a range of strategies to stay on the right track. Adolescents with access to a car will often volunteer to be the designated driver so that they can easily decline alcohol or drugs. Others blame their teetotaling on a prescription that can't mix with booze, a family history of substance misuse, or iron-fisted parents who will ship them off to military school if they step out of line. To be clear, what teenagers tell their peers in the interest of staying safe need not be true. But it should be nailed down before they head into hot cognition minefields where they're unlikely to do their best thinking.

Using cold cognition to make sure teens have workable safety plans that can be implemented in hot cognition settings cannot, of course, guarantee that nothing will go wrong. Nor can adults anticipate every risk that an adolescent might take. My parents, for their part, didn't even know that skitching was a thing. All the same, understanding how social contexts influence teenage reasoning around risk can help us, and our teenagers, work with the fact that adolescent emotions can, at times, undermine good judgment.

## Myth #2: Difficult Emotions Are Bad for Teens

In addition to caring for teenagers in my private practice, I spend part of each week working with various schools and their students. I have been a longtime consultant at Laurel School, a PK-12 girls' school in Cleveland, and speaking opportunities have brought me into close contact with a wide range of other schools around the country and the world. I love working with educators and count many of them among my closest colleagues and friends. So it was hardly unusual when, on a Monday morning in early fall, I received a friendly text from the principal of a public middle school in the Northeast.

"Got a minute?" she asked by text.

"You bet," I replied. "Is now good?"

It was, and after we'd checked in briefly about our families and our summers, she said, "I'm getting a lot of pushback from some parents about our eighth grade English assignments. A lot of what's on the list is standard fare, *To Kill a Mockingbird* and the like, but we've added several new books because we want to vary the authors and perspectives we present."

"The parents you're hearing from—what are they taking issue with?"

"They're bothered by the fact that some of the content is very upsetting. I get it. There's some pretty tough stuff in the novels they read, but these are stories about things that are happening, or really did happen. And they were vetted by our librarian, who has a really good feel for what's developmentally appropriate."

"Are you hearing concerns just about what they're reading in English, or is it coming up in other subjects, too?" I asked.

"Some parents don't like our social studies unit on Jim Crow, but it seems to be a bigger deal in English. One mom said that she doesn't mind when we present dry historical facts, but she felt it wasn't good for kids to be made to read emotionally intense stories that bring those facts to life."

"Oh!" I said, feeling somewhat taken aback by the strength of the parents' response to disquieting books. "Well, I'm not quite sure what you should say to the folks you're hearing from, but I can tell you that you have the research on your side."

From there I explained that several psychological studies have confirmed that reading helps to foster empathy. Far from being harmful to teenagers, reading compelling narratives of lived experiences builds compassion and the ability to take another person's perspective. Perhaps most interesting, research shows that this effect is achieved only when young people become emotionally engaged with what they are reading. Dry historical facts don't work the same magic. Empathy builds in teenagers only when literature stirs their feelings. This point was made eloquently by Mary Ann Evans Cross, better known by her pen name, George Eliot, who observed that "The greatest benefit we owe the artist, whether painter, poet, or novelist, is the extension of our sympathies."

There is, without question, developmental value in reading evocative accounts of other people's lives, even when their stories trouble us greatly. That said, I'm a mom myself and I know how hard it is to see one's child wrestle with strong, unsettling emotions. I can easily understand why parents might wonder if being exposed to such distressing content at school is really necessary. But I know that in the long run it's good for young people to experience powerful emotions, even ones that knock them off balance.

I said to my friend, "Parents tend to have good instincts about what their kids can and can't handle, so I'd be open to their questions about what's being assigned. That said, so long as the books are age-appropriate, are read with the help of a thoughtful teacher, and are accompanied by meaningful class discussions, I would say that engaging with stories that inspire uncomfortable emotions is not too much to ask of most kids. In fact, it plays a critical role in helping young people grow."

## Emotional Discomfort Promotes Growth

Emotional pain promotes maturation. This is true when it is inspired by arts and literature, and likely even more true when it comes from difficult personal experiences. I first started to wrap my head around this idea when I was a postdoctoral fellow at a training clinic at the University of Michigan. The clinic served adults in the local area, and I was assigned a thirty-year-old client who, in our intake interview, made it clear that she drank a lot. As I relayed the details of our first session to my supervisor, a senior psychologist on the clinic's teaching faculty, he stopped me at the part about her alcohol use. "You need to find out how old she was when she started drinking heavily," he said, "because people stop maturing at the point when they start abusing substances."

I reflected on those words for weeks. It seemed to me impossible that such a generic comment could be true across the board. Over time, however, I came to understand what my supervisor was talking about and to appreciate that he was imparting wisdom long understood by clinicians specializing in the treatment of substance misuse.

Here's the reality: Feeling the emotional impact of difficult experiences helps us to grow up. Picture a teenager who gets caught cheating on a test at school. She'll have to face painful consequences for her actions, such as getting a zero on the test and receiving any other punishment doled out by the school or at home. She's likely to feel guilty about having cheated, and perhaps about having disappointed her parents and her teachers. All of this will help her to reflect on the kind of person she wants to be. As much as we would not want our child to go through an experience like this, teenagers and parents often come to regard such a crisis as a meaningful turning point in a young person's life.

Or think of a boy who gets dumped by his girlfriend. He may be devastated, struggle to get out of bed, and live under a cloud for days. But if his misery inspires him to seek and accept support from good friends, reflect on what worked in the relationship and what didn't, and discover that he can weather more psychological discomfort than he realized, the breakup can become a growth-giving (if still profoundly unwanted) experience.

When substances come into the mix, however, maturation halts. Whatever else can be said about drugs and alcohol, they are very good at blocking emotional pain, and therefore the maturation that comes with it. If the girl who cheats on her test gets high to numb her discomfort, she may find her way through the ordeal, but she won't learn from it. If the boy who gets dumped by his girlfriend drinks to blunt his heartache until it eventually fades or he finds someone new, he'll miss a key opportunity to deepen his understanding of himself and his relationships.

Okay, I know. The idea that experiencing psychological distress helps teens to mature may sound great in theory, but it's another story when your own child is feeling emotional pain. Caring parents hate to see their kids suffer and become understandably worried when their teens are undone. So what's a loving adult to do?

In the first place, we can try to notice when we are going out of our way to keep a teen from becoming upset. It's easy to fall into this trap. With a great deal of life experience to draw on, we can often anticipate difficulties that our teenagers don't seem to realize might be headed their way. We see a problem looming and want to move our teenagers out of its path, in an attempt to cash in our well-earned wisdom for their benefit.

I think here of a friend of mine who shared that her family meals had become tense as her son's high school soccer season approached. My friend's well-meaning wife was often using dinnertime to ask their fifteen-year-old son about his progress with getting in shape for tryouts. The boy bristled at her efforts to get him going on his training regimen, as one would expect from any normally developing teenager, and the meals often ended in an angry argument or a stony silence. "I know she means well," my friend said of her spouse, "but it's making life at home really miserable." She went on to explain that she'd asked her wife why she kept bringing up a topic that invariably ruined their meals. "She's worried that he'll be crushed if he gets cut from the team. Which I understand—he definitely will be."

My friend wondered about their options. Was there a chance that if her wife kept asking about their son's conditioning plans he might become more receptive to her guidance? "This already isn't working," I said to her. "Doing *more* of it is probably a bad idea." Instead, I suggested that they might articulate their dilemma to their son. They could say, "We love you and know how much you want to make the soccer team, and we all know that you can stack the deck in your favor by getting in shape now." And then leave it at that.

A third option would be to stop talking about it and let the soccer chips fall where they may. "To do this," I pointed out, "your wife will have to accept that he may have a really hard time with it—either when he gets to tryouts and realizes that he's struggling to keep up, or because he gets cut." Biting your tongue is not easy to do. But we need to remember that a lesson learned the hard way is still a lesson learned.

What if he doesn't make the team and is beside himself about it? How should the boy's parents respond? Saying or signaling "I told you so" can be very tempting, but it's not the best way to go. Instead, we should embrace the reality that being presented with a teenager who is intensely distressed—for any reason at all—opens the door to what may be the best use of our middle-age wisdom. When teenagers become distraught, it is all but impossible for them to maintain a sense of perspective. If there's one good thing that comes with middle age, it's perspective. At fifteen, getting cut from the soccer team feels like the end of the world. North of thirty-five, we know that it's not.

Putting our hard-earned perspective to use for our teens means walking a delicate line. On the one hand, we want to communicate to our teenagers that regardless of how awful the situation feels right now, life will go on and they will soon feel better. On the other, we want to validate the fact of their suffering. The best way to pull off this balancing act is to project a sense of calm. This can be hard to do. When our kids become upset, we feel upset too; there's a lot of truth to the adage that "You're only as happy as your least happy child."

It matters, however, that we serve as a steady presence for our teenagers whenever they become overwrought. We can do this by listening intently and patiently when our teens want to talk about what's wrong. And for those who don't feel like talking, we can lend our support by gently offering a favorite beverage, our quiet company, or an invitation to watch their favorite movie. Remaining calm when teenagers become undone communicates the critical point that we are not frightened by their acute discomfort, and so they don't need to be frightened by it either.

Of course, just because we put on a brave face for our kids doesn't mean that we're not feeling their hurts. At times like this, it's helpful for parents to have others to lean on for support, perhaps an empathetic friend, a loving adult sibling, a trusted colleague, or all of the above. Further, reminding ourselves that going through difficult experiences almost always helps our teens grow can make it easier for us to bear their distress. Finally, we should remember that, while emotions are sometimes painful, they are rarely harmful.

### When Should Teens Be Shielded from Emotional Pain?

Teenagers are built to withstand a great deal of discomfort and to mature as they do so. We need to worry about lasting damage from an event only if it crosses the line from disquieting to traumatic. Let's take a close look at that line.

The term "trauma" has found its way into our everyday language. It is now used to describe not only frightening or physically harmful events, such as a car accident or a mugging, but also troubling but not life-threatening events, such as getting stranded at the airport or watching your favorite sports team lose a game in the final seconds. When mental health professionals use the term, however, we have a very specific definition in mind. For us, "trauma" refers to the overwhelming *emotional impact* of a horrible event, never to the event itself.

This may seem like splitting hairs, but the distinction is an important one. Here's why: It happens all the time that the exact same event traumatizes one person but not another. In the eyes of psychologists, trauma occurs when an individual suffers greater emotional stress than that person can find a way to tolerate.

Imagine, for example, two teenage boys who get lost while hiking, spend a scary night in the woods wondering if they'll ever be found, and are rescued in the morning. In this kind of situation, it would not be unusual for one boy to come away from the expe-

rience feeling profoundly upset, and for the other boy to be traumatized. The first boy was somehow able to mentally withstand
the experience, to find a way to cope with the dread caused by
getting lost in the woods. In contrast, the second boy's coping
abilities were totally outmatched by the force of his psychological suffering. It is the difference between a dam that is tested by a
surge of water but ultimately holds, and another that is burst by
the same surge. Though both boys went through an awful experience, the first boy was frightened, while the second was overwhelmed and thus traumatized.

Mental health experts study trauma carefully, because trau-
matization is more than just worrisome; it can actually cause
lasting neurological harm. Research shows that emotionally
traumatizing experiences sometimes damage the functioning of
the nervous system, specifically a component known as the HPA
(hypothalamic-pituitary-adrenal) axis. When we feel scared, the
hypothalamus, a structure in the brain that processes emotions,
sets off a cascading biological reaction. It activates the pituitary
gland, which in turn activates the adrenal gland, which then re-
leases stress hormones, such as adrenaline and cortisol, into the
bloodstream. The activation of the HPA axis causes feelings of
restlessness and anxiety that, according to evolutionary design,
should help us deal with the threat that started the whole process. Most of the time, the HPA axis reacts in proportion to the
peril, and, once the danger passes, resets to its resting state.

Experiencing trauma, especially during critical periods of development, can harm the cells that regulate the HPA axis. One
study measured the hormonal response of research participants
as they engaged in the stressful task of speaking to an audience
while catheters collected blood samples before, during, and after
their speeches. Of the research participants, half had been abused
as children and half had not. The research participants who had
been maltreated when they were young released stress hormones

in an amount six times greater than those who had not endured maltreatment. In short, traumatizing experiences can lead to lasting hyperactivity in the HPA axis, and, along with it, chronically elevated anxiety and an outsized fear reaction to everyday stressors.

Not everyone who is traumatized goes on to have lasting difficulties. At times, however, trauma can lead to PTSD, the psychological diagnosis given to some of the war veterans in the reasoning studies we considered earlier. PTSD is characterized by horrendous, ongoing symptoms that include intrusive memories of the traumatic event, agitation, numbness, hypervigilance, withdrawal, and estrangement from oneself and others.

So here's the bottom line: We don't want to shield our teenagers from intense, growth-promoting emotions, but we don't want them to encounter situations that could cause trauma. Whether an individual is traumatized by a harrowing event comes down to several factors including past experiences, psychological health prior to the event, the quality of the social support on hand, and even genetic vulnerabilities. Some events are so dreadful—rape, severe abuse, near-death experiences, the ravages of war—that trauma can all but be assumed among those who survive such ordeals, because few humans come equipped to withstand horrors of that magnitude. But most experiences fall into a gray area in which they are psychologically overwhelming for some people but not for others.

How, you might be wondering, are loving parents to know when a teenager is facing a situation that might cross the line from troublesome to traumatic? The answer depends on the adolescent in question. To return to the example of emotionally profound reading material, the same novel that helps one teenager build empathy might overwhelm another teenager who has limited resources for managing distress. We might also keep a special eye out for situations that could hit too close to home for a young person who has suffered an unusually painful event. A thoughtful principal I know was aware that one of her eighth graders had lost her father to suicide. She reached out to the student's mother to alert her that a story was being assigned that involved a character who kills himself. Together they weighed the book's appropriateness for the student. Ultimately, the mother decided to ask the girl if she wanted to read the story, given that it included a suicide. The girl did elect to read it, but only after asking her teacher to tell her the whole story first.

While adolescents benefit from learning how to swim through choppy emotional waters, they should never be allowed to feel as though they're drowning. You know your child, should trust your assessment, and should guard against stressful situations that might overpower your teen's coping resources.

If you know that you, your child, or someone you love has been traumatized, seek care from a clinician who has specialized training in this area. In the last several decades we've made tremendous strides in addressing trauma and PTSD with treatments such as psychotherapy, mindfulness practices, medications, and yoga. Such support is greatly warranted and can significantly reduce suffering.

## Myth #3: With Their Amped-Up Emotions, Teens Are Psychologically Fragile

Not long ago, I gave a presentation to parents at a high school in Minnesota, only to discover right after the talk that one of my college classmates was in the audience. He waited until I had answered the last question from the audience, then came and found me in the back of the auditorium. Though I remembered him as a carefree and fun-loving college student, it was clear that he had grown into a serious, earnest adult and the devoted father of three girls, ages twelve, fourteen, and sixteen. After catching up about our families and our jobs, we exchanged contact information and resolved to stay in touch.

Six months later, I heard from him by email. "Hey, I hope you're good!" he wrote. "And I hope it's okay for me to ask—please let me know if it's not—but I'm wondering if I can get your advice about my oldest daughter, Lucia. She sometimes seems really down and I'm not sure how worried to be or what to do." I told him that I was glad he had reached out, and we found a time to talk.

My friend explained over the phone that Lucia was an ambitious, hard-driving high school junior. "She works like a machine and is doing well academically but sometimes says she feels like a failure." My friend shared that his daughter had lately been dissolving into tears two or even three nights a week and had once said that she "just wants to give up." He added, "It's hard to know what to think. Often, Lucia seems like her old self—she's happy and energetic. Then the next day she's really low and I wonder if she might be depressed. And then there are times when she cracks jokes about feeling overwhelmed—she tells us that she's going to drop out of school and support herself by selling friendship bracelets. She's a fun kid with a great sense of humor, but I don't always know what to make of her ups and downs. I'm wondering if we need to take her to a psychologist or have her cut back on her commitments, or do something else altogether. I don't want to overreact, but I don't want to underreact, either—especially if something's really wrong."

After empathizing with my friend's concerns and acknowledging how unsettling it can be to have a teenager drop comments that sound hopeless, I asked several questions to rule out the possibility that Lucia suffered from depression. My friend confirmed that she was sleeping and eating normally, that she continued to enjoy watching her favorite shows on the weekend and spending time with her friends. He confirmed that there was always a legitimate explanation when she felt down or became tearful. "Sometimes it's because she's gotten a low grade, or she has a really heavy night of homework," he explained, "but she always rallies that night or the next morning." I asked if she was highly irritable—a symptom of depression that is far more common in adolescents than adults—to which he responded tenderly, "She's no more irritable than I remember being as a teenager."

I was able to reassure my friend that it did not sound to me as though Lucia was depressed. She was, however, experiencing the pronounced mood swings that tend to come with adolescence. Regarding her comment about wanting to "give up," I let him know that it's not unusual for teenagers to use alarming language to describe a short-lived rush of despair. When this happens, the best response is to ask her what she really means. "Are you having thoughts about hurting yourself," he could say, "or are you just letting me know how upset you feel right now?" If Lucia shares that she's thinking about self-harm, he should circle back to me or her pediatrician for guidance. If, as is more likely, she clarifies that she is feeling deeply unhappy but poses no risk to herself, he should turn the conversation to whatever is bothering her.

"That makes sense," said my friend, "and is something I can definitely do." Then he added, "There's something else—and my wife has noticed it too. It often seems like Lucia feels better once she dumps her distress on us. For instance, she'll make some off-handed comment that leaves me feeling concerned—like saying that she feels hopeless about ever finding someone to date—and the next thing I know, she's headed out to have fun with her friends."

"Ah," I responded. "What you're describing is pretty common among teenagers. Unloading painful feelings onto their parents is one of the many ways that teens manage their intense emotions. When they do this, our worries can really get going. But teens are usually sturdier than they seem."

### Emotional Does Not Mean Fragile

With teenagers, it's easy to mistake emotionality for fragility. Given how intense adolescent moods can be, parents often worry that what they're seeing are signs of real psychological trouble. Allow me to offer reassurance on three different grounds.

First, teens often carry themselves differently at home than they do out in the world. They usually hold themselves together quite ably at school, at practices and rehearsals, or at their jobs, all the while absorbing frustrations, hurt feelings, and disappointments with equanimity and grace. Then, once they return home and are with us, they can finally let themselves fall apart. In many ways, this is an excellent system. Knowing that they can be insecure and vulnerable at home usually allows our teenagers to be collected and operate with more confidence when they're out and about. As parents, we should bear in mind that we rarely see the complete picture of our teenager's overall psychological sturdiness.

Second, if you're feeling concerned about your teenager's ups and downs, remember our guiding definition of mental health, one that we'll keep coming back to throughout this book. Mental health is not about feeling good. Instead, it's about having the right feelings at the right time and being able to manage those feelings effectively. Not that there's such a thing as a "wrong" feeling; what we're getting at here is whether emotions make sense and are proportional given the situation. Lucia was becoming upset for upsetting reasons, and she found adaptive approaches to help herself feel better, such as breaking down in tears. Though we hate to see our kids sobbing, it's helpful to remember that there really is such a thing as a "good cry." Both everyday experience and carefully conducted studies suggest that a period of weeping typically gives way to a general sense of emotional relief. This certainly seemed to be the case for Lucia, who, as her dad explained, would "rally" shortly after melting down.

Third, parents don't need to worry that a highly moody adolescent is nearing a breaking point because teenagers, like all of us, come with protective defense mechanisms that, like circuit breakers, automatically help combat emotional overload. For instance, Lucia sometimes mobilized the widely recognized psychological defense of humor—joking about dropping out of school and selling friendship bracelets—to discharge some of her discomfort.

When emotions threaten to become too high-voltage, every one of us has defenses that kick in to reduce their charge. These defenses that help us buffer intense emotions are unconscious, meaning that we summon them without even realizing that we have done so. There are a variety of defenses that people rely on, but not all defenses are equally good for us. What makes some defenses better than others? The higher-quality psychological defenses distort reality the least. The less adaptive ones blunt psychological distress by messing with the truth. In this sense, *humor* is a high-quality defense. We often feel better about a bad situation when we can joke about it, but kidding around about a painful reality doesn't mean we've lost touch with the truth of it. *Denial,* on the other hand, is not a healthy defense: Insisting that a rapidly spreading rash isn't a problem might reduce anxiety about what's causing it, but only by sacrificing the truth.

It's important that we and our teenagers find ways to withstand painful feelings without warping reality. Having one's psychological comfort hinge on a distorted version of the truth undermines the possibility of engaging meaningfully with the world and the people in it.

Most of the time, teenagers use healthy defenses to manage troubling feelings. For example, often they arrive at constructive outlets for an unwanted emotion, a defense we call *sublimation*. One teenager might redirect her anger at her brother into her softball pitch, another might channel his sadness over his grandmother's death into an evocative painting.

At other times, teenagers come up with justifications that make a bad situation more bearable, the defense known as *rationalization*. If a girl's longtime crush starts dating someone else, she might tell herself that it's probably better to spend her time with friends she'll have forever than with a boyfriend she'll need to break up with when it's time to go to college.

Some kinds of defenses are prominent at particular points in life. Babies, for example, come equipped with rudimentary defense systems and rely on simple *withdrawal* when they feel overwhelmed. They close their eyes if someone gets too close, and they tend to fall asleep quickly when brought along to dinner at a loud restaurant. If there's one defense that teenagers specialize in, it's what psychologists refer to as *externalization*. This defense is managing an unpleasant emotion by getting someone else (often a loving parent) to feel it instead. Lucia's father captured externalization perfectly when he observed that once his daughter said something that left him feeling shaken, she often seemed to feel quite a bit better. Think of externalization as handing off emotional trash. A teenager who no longer wants to carry around an unwanted feeling sometimes finds a way to dump it on a caring, but perhaps unsuspecting, adult.

Externalization is at work when a teenager sends an alarming dispatch from school—perhaps texting "I think I just screwed up my big math test"—and then goes dark when the garbage-collecting parent texts back with anxious questions. In all likelihood, the teen felt relief as soon as he handed off his worries about the test and now may have no interest in discussing it further. The parent may feel weighed down by the bad news, but the teen, having tossed off the concern about the test, can focus on the rest of his day.

So, is externalization a healthy defense? Yes, insofar as it buffers an adolescent's distress without warping reality. When teens use externalization as a defense, they don't deny the problem at hand or blame it on anyone else. They simply communicate about it in a way that leaves their parents feeling lousy. This may work well enough for the teenager, but there's no question that it's really not much fun to be the adult on the receiving end of an externalization.

Should this happen to you (as it almost certainly has or will), there are several ways to feel better about it. For one, appreciate that externalization is actually a form of communication. Instead of *telling* us how they feel, externalizing teenagers help us understand their emotional lives by *making* us feel what they do. This might ruin your evening, but it can also help you empathize with just how worried, scared, or frustrated your teenager feels. For another, you can consider emotional garbage collection to be among the loving services you provide to your teenager. Coming of age brings with it a world of emotional intensity. Getting to periodically unload some of that emotion onto an adult who cares enough to take the feeling seriously is a real help. Last, keep in mind that externalizing a problem often helps a teen solve it. Shifting the emotional weight of a bad situation onto you may free up your son to address the situation from a practical perspective, such as checking in with his math teacher to ask about options for retaking the test.

Here's the key point: Normally developing teenagers experience pronounced highs and lows, but that is not, in and of itself, reason to be worried that they are falling apart. We can be confident in their overall emotional health so long as three things are true: Adolescents should have *feelings that make sense* in light of their circumstances; they should find *adaptive ways to manage* those emotions (such as having a good cry); and they should *rely on a range of defenses* that offer relief without distorting reality.

## When Is Professional Support in Order?

There may, of course, be a time when a teenager needs professional psychological support. How will we know if that time has come? We can start by considering whether an adolescent's feelings make sense. It's time to worry when a teenager's emotions don't add up. This simple measure can, for example, help us distinguish between sadness and clinical depression or between healthy and unhealthy anxiety.

Let's begin with the difference between sadness and clinical depression. When young people suffer losses or disappointments, we fully expect them to be unhappy. We regard a period of low mood as evidence that their emotions are in proper working order. In contrast, people who feel sad or numb without explanation may be suffering from clinical depression. We also suspect depression if a distressing event that should cause a *transient* sense of sadness, such as a good friend's moving away, leads instead to a pervasive and lasting bleakness. Put simply, you probably don't need to be worried if your teenager is sad about *something* for a little while; you should be concerned if your teen is sad about *everything* for days at a time.

It's the same with anxiety. You may not have expected to see anxiety just mentioned as an emotion that can be healthy. In recent years, anxiety, along with every other unpleasant emotion, has gotten an unnecessarily bad rap. In fact, psychologists have long understood anxiety to be a healthy, protective alarm that alerts us to threats. These threats can be on the outside, such as when a teenager realizes that the road he's driving on has become icy, or on the inside, such as when a teenager realizes that he's a week behind on studying for an upcoming test. Feeling anxious on icy roads or when procrastinating can focus a teen's attention usefully, motivating him to drive with care or to hit the books. Back to our simple measure, clinicians consider anxiety to be unhealthy only when it doesn't make sense, either because it's ringing the alarm when there's nothing to worry about, or the scale of the anxiety is way out of proportion to the threat. In other words, we wouldn't want a person to feel anxious when driving under safe conditions. And though a teen *should* be nervous if he's not prepared for a test, if his anxiety caused panic attacks, it would be out of proportion. Anxiety that fits the situation is one thing, anxiety that doesn't is another.

Next, we should also pay attention to whether teenagers are managing their feelings in adaptive ways. In the case of the girl who feels down because a good friend has moved away, her sad feelings are not themselves grounds for concern. But it's time to worry if she deals with her misery by turning to harmful strategies: getting high, becoming excessively short-tempered with her parents, or pushing other friends away. For sure, even the most psychologically sturdy adolescents do not always handle their feelings well. But when teens make a habit of seeking emotional relief in ways that are risky or costly, it's time to be concerned.

We should also notice when teenagers rely on unhealthy psychological defenses to manage painful feelings. As we know, the unhealthy defenses buffer uncomfortable emotions by compromising reality, such as when a person insists that a painful event never occurred (denial), has no memory of something awful that really did happen (repression), or feels entirely disconnected from her or his own thoughts, feelings, or body (dissociation). Defenses that distort reality are most likely to arise from terrible or traumatizing experiences and strongly suggest the need for psychological support. Indeed, some parents become aware that their teenager may have suffered a trauma only when the teen begins to rely on unhealthy defenses to try to keep the psychological aftermath of the trauma at bay.

As much as it can be helpful to have guidelines for when to worry about your adolescent's emotional health, you don't have to figure this out on your own. If you're wondering whether your teenager needs professional psychological support—and *especially* if your teen has feelings that don't add up, is handling emotions poorly, or is relying on unhealthy defenses—reach out to a mental health professional for advice on next steps.

What about teenagers who mention feeling suicidal or who talk about wanting to hurt themselves? Such comments should *always* be taken seriously. As a first step, you should ask if the teen would ever act on these words, as I coached Lucia's father to do. If you get an answer that does not leave you completely reassured, seek help right away from a health professional, such as the teen's pediatrician, or—if you are concerned about your teen's immediate safety—take your teenager to an emergency room. What if teens aren't mentioning suicide, but adults have reason to worry that it might be on their minds? Again, ask. Say, "I understand that this question may seem a little bit out of the blue, but given how upset you are, I feel that I need to ask it—have you had any thoughts about hurting yourself or ending your life?" Adults sometimes avoid the topic of suicide because they worry that bringing it up will cause teenagers to feel even more uneasy. To the contrary, research shows that asking nonsuicidal teens about suicide does not leave them feeling worse, but for teens who *are* feeling suicidal, it relieves distress.

Experts have long studied the factors that put teens at higher risk for taking their own lives and for years have been working from the understanding that the prime risk factors to look for are depression, anxiety, substance use, or other psychiatric disorders. These are indeed major risk factors for adolescent suicide, but we recently learned that they mostly apply to white adolescents. Unfortunately, the profession of psychology has a long history of taking a one-size-fits-all approach to its research findings. Once our results are in, we work from the assumption that they apply equally to individuals from a wide range of racial, ethnic, and socioeconomic backgrounds. And that's not always correct.

One stark example relates to Black adolescents and suicide. While the suicide rate among teenagers has, alarmingly, been on the rise in recent decades, the latest data reveal that the most dramatic upticks have occurred among Black teens. When experts turned to the research literature to make sense of this trend, they came up all but empty-handed, because until recently we have not studied whether Black adolescents face risk factors of their own. So when the suicide rate among Black teens started to stand out from the general trend, we had no idea why, or what to do about it.

Thankfully, as a result of research fast-tracked by a congressional emergency caucus and the National Institute of Mental Health, the picture has started to come into focus. Early findings indicate that much of what we know about suicide in white teenagers does not extend to Black adolescents. Compared to their white counterparts, Black teens who died by suicide were less likely to have a known mental health problem or to have shared their suicidal thoughts or plans. They were, however, more likely to have recently experienced a crisis, a family problem, or an argument, and were also more likely to have made past suicide attempts.

With more representative data, we're better equipped to know what to look for and when to worry about the safety of Black youth. This emerging information also provides further evidence of the systemic racial disparities in health care. The fact that Black teens were *less* likely than white teens to have known mental health problems yet were *more* likely to have made past suicide attempts highlights the fact that, on the whole, Black teenagers and their families are severely underserved by mental health services.

The emotional lives of teenagers cannot be divorced from the social forces that shape their world. And the social forces that shape their world are determined by the different identities that teens carry. Some young people come of age while contending constantly with racism, discrimination, and marginalization, which weigh upon not only their emotional lives but also their aspirations, physical safety, and access to care. As we consider how young people navigate and come to terms with their emotions, we must also acknowledge this reality.

So far, what have we established about the emotional lives of our teenagers? First, their emotions provide valuable information and have a place at the decision-making table. Second, it is not our goal to protect adolescents from unwanted emotions, because those emotions play an important role in maturation. And third, adults shouldn't mistake the extreme emotional intensity that is natural to adolescence for psychological fragility. Putting it all together, we want our teenagers to appreciate the input provided by their feelings, to know that uncomfortable experiences will help them grow, and to learn how to navigate their emotions effectively.

With these ideas as our mainstays, let's go on to discuss the forces that shape psychological development in young people, and how we can support our teenagers as they build healthy, enriching emotional lives that will carry them into adulthood. The first stop? One of the most powerful forces shaping adolescents' emotional lives: gender.

■ ■ ■ ■ ■

## CHAPTER TWO

# Gender and Emotion

Zach, a lanky high school sophomore, sat drooping on my office couch. He had come for his regular Thursday afternoon appointment, but it looked as though he would much rather be at home in his bed.

"You seem pretty tired," I said, matter-of-factly.

"Yeah," he said, "I was up really late."

"How come?"

"I played World of Warcraft until two this morning."

Though I often care for adolescent girls in my practice, I am also referred teenaged boys and am always glad to see them. They tend to bring a different energy than girls, but when they are struggling with their emotions, I can count on the same fundamental, universal questions that always guide my clinical work: Are they having the right feeling at the right time—does the emotion make sense in its context? Are they managing their feelings effectively?

One thing I know about boys is to take seriously the role that gaming sometimes plays in their emotional lives. Zach was both a conscientious student and a dedicated athlete, and I knew that it was not like him to stay up late on a weeknight playing online games. I strongly suspected that something had stirred Zach up and he had turned to his game for relief.

"What time did you start playing?"

"About eleven."

Hoping to get to the bottom of things, I asked, "Were you done with your homework?" while trying to sound not the least bit judgmental.

"Yeah, I was done. I was texting with Mara and heading to bed. I didn't really mean to start playing—and then once I did, I lost track of time."

"How's Mara?" I asked. Mara was a girl he'd been mentioning lately, also a tenth grader at his school. He had shared that he liked her and that they had made out on a few occasions. Recently, she had been raising questions about the exact status of their relationship.

"She's fine . . . I guess . . . I dunno," he said, with an edge of discomfort creeping into his voice. "Last night she asked if I was hooking up with anyone else, or just her."

"What did you say?"

"I don't think I answered . . . that's about when I started playing World of Warcraft."

Zach quickly moved on to new topics—tomorrow's test, an upcoming swim meet—and replicated in my office the same coping mechanisms he'd relied on the night before. Faced with an uneasy emotion, he found a distraction. Last night it was World of Warcraft, today in my office it was a change of subject.

As Zach talked about the big test he had the next day, I'll confess that my mind wandered. I started to think about Mara and what the previous night might have looked like for her. I assumed that she was unsettled by Zach's abrupt disappearance from their text thread, especially when she had just asked a question about the nature of their relationship. Did she wait up for a reply? Had she started to worry when nothing came through? Might she have called a friend to try to process Zach's sudden silence? Did she share a screenshot of the conversation in a group text so that several friends could give it a close reading and offer feedback on where she might have screwed up? Given what I know about girls, these all seemed likely possibilities.

Why? Because when it comes to managing emotional distress, boys are more likely to turn to distraction, and girls are more likely to turn to discussion.

## Why Gender Differences Matter

Well, that was certainly a sweeping generalization! "Boys distract, girls discuss." What should we make of statements like that, especially given that our understanding of gender has changed so dramatically in recent years? Do such broad gender claims really hold up? No. And also yes. Let's start with the no. There are four big ways that gender differences, especially emotion-related ones of the sort we're addressing, are exaggerated.

First, no matter how you slice it, females and males are vastly more alike than they are different. Even when we can identify clear gender distinctions, the differences *within* any one gender are far greater than the average differences *between* the genders. For example, men tend to be taller than women, but the height difference between the shortest man and the tallest is far greater than the difference between the average heights of men and women. This is also true for psychological differences: If you want to see the greatest variety, look within a single gender group rather than comparing groups.

Second, we should bear in mind that whenever gender disparities are identified, it's still the group averages we're talking about. Very few individual human beings sit at the exact average point. This means that even though the "average boy" is more physically aggressive than the "average girl," plenty of girls are *more* aggressive than the average boy, and plenty of boys are *less* aggressive than the average girl. This also explains why your particular teenager may not fit every gendered stereotype that you hear bandied about. And it means that if I offer a description of a gendered behavior that doesn't apply to your teen, or if your teen doesn't identify with the traditional male/female gender binary, ignore the fact that I've presented a "boy issue" or a "girl issue" and focus on the issue itself.

Third, we should never assume that psychological gender differences are entirely innate. Though clear differences around how boys and girls handle emotion start to emerge in childhood, these gendered patterns are overwhelmingly the result of socialization. Wittingly or not, we *teach* girls one way to respond to emotion, and boys another. These differences may become ingrained, but they aren't inevitable.

Fourth, today's teens have a different perspective on gender than the adolescents of generations past. They are less likely to see gender in terms of hard-and-fast male/female categories, or to feel compelled to fulfill traditional gender roles. For them, psychological gender differences have shallower roots than they did for their parents and grandparents. While most of this chapter addresses traditional gender categories, we'll also consider the emotional experiences of adolescents for whom these categories don't fit.

So, if generalizations about gender differences are limited in so many ways, why should we pay attention to them at all?

There are two good reasons. One is that we *do* observe real, measurable disparities in how girls and boys, in general, conduct themselves around their emotions. These population-level differences shape our teenagers' daily experiences and the world they must negotiate. The other reason is that any thoughtful look at emotional gender differences is above all a consideration of where those differences come from, and of where and how we might address them in the interest of providing our teens fuller, healthier emotional lives.

So, with that in mind, let's mine emotional gender differences for what they're worth.

## Gender Rules Start Early

Being identified as either female or male comes with being handed an already wrapped package of expectations around emotion. As soon as parents learn the sex of their baby, many begin to form an image of their future child in their imagination. They may assume that their daughter will be sensitive and moody, and their son will be assertive and tough. These assumptions influence how we respond to our children's expressions of emotion and in turn shape how children learn to communicate their feelings.

At birth, boys actually tend to be moodier than girls. They're generally fussier, given to crying, and harder to soothe. But by the time kids hit school, boys are not as outwardly emotional as girls. Compared to girls, they are less likely to display both positive and negative feelings. They smile less and exhibit lower levels of happiness than girls do. They are also less likely to openly express sadness or anxiety. The narrowing of boys' emotional repertoire happens quickly. One remarkable study found that between preschool and the end of first grade, boys' expressions of sadness and anxiety dropped by 50 percent while girls' held steady. In fact, among school-aged children there are only two feelings that boys show more frequently than girls: anger, and pleasure that comes at someone else's expense.

How do our sons and daughters end up in two different emotional ballparks? We often have parenting to thank. Whether we mean to or not, from day one we subtly help children adopt the gendered emotional scripts established by our broader culture. We do this in part by responding to expressions of emotion that match gendered stereotypes and ignoring the ones that don't. Our young children want our attention more than anything else, and they quickly figure out to do more of the behaviors that get us to tune in and fewer of the behaviors that make us tune out. Research shows that parents are more comfortable with their daughters expressing fear and their sons expressing anger than the other way around. And parents are more likely to turn their attention elsewhere when their sons feel sad and anxious, and when their daughters become angry.

In addition to shaping behavior with how we react to kids' emotion, we also use direct instruction. Parents tend to encourage their sons to limit "unnecessary" crying, to get their feelings under control, and not to show fear. In contrast, when our daughters are sad or scared, we tend to talk with them about what's wrong and how it might be fixed. In a similar vein, parents are more likely to urge their sons to cope with distress by distraction—to just "not think about it" or "focus on something else"—and to help their daughters feel better by encouraging them to share what's on their mind.

Once this gendered emotional code takes hold, it has powerful implications for how young people manage their feelings over time. As I learned in my office, Zach dampened his discomfort about Mara's question by losing himself in an online game, and it was easy for me to picture Mara reaching out to her friends to talk about her perplexing interaction with Zach.

## Gender Differences in Empathy and Aggression

Gender differences don't just influence how young people cope with their own feelings—they shape how teenagers respond to other people's emotions as well. Research consistently finds that teenage girls demonstrate more empathy than teenage boys. Girls are better able to imagine other people's perspectives and to accurately decode the feelings behind their facial expressions. Girls are also more likely than boys to go out of their way to be helpful when they perceive that another person is in need. Again, plenty of teenage boys are more empathetic than the average teenage girl, and many teenage girls are less empathetic than the average teenage boy; but girls, *on average*, demonstrate more empathy than boys do. For why this is true, we have a range of explanations.

Animal studies suggest that there may be an evolutionary reason for the females of a species to be stronger in the empathy department. From a gene propagation perspective, the females in a species are more likely to stay close to home caring for their contributions to the gene pool, while their male counterparts are more likely to be out and about spreading their genes.

If this theory strikes you as an oversimplification, believe me, I am right there with you. Darwinian takes on modern human behavior tend to get my hackles up, because they often sound like nothing more than justifications for guys to sleep around. That said, I've included the evolutionary explanation of the empathy gap here because my wish to provide an even-handed account of the psychological science outweighs (just barely) my wish to suppress evidence I find annoying.

Fortunately, there are other explanations, too. When our kids are being unkind, we are more likely to correct our daughters by encouraging them to imagine how their actions might make other people feel, while we're more likely to bring our sons in line by way of verbal threats or physical punishments. One particularly fascinating study looked at how parents use school-related conversations to signal how much they do, or don't, expect their kids to think about other people. Recording after-school exchanges between mothers and their kindergarteners, researchers found that the mothers in their study were more likely to ask sons about learning-related topics and to ask their daughters about their interactions with their classmates and teachers. Assuming there is an evolutionary seed of truth that helps explain why girls are more empathetic than boys, the empathy gap we see in adolescence serves as a good example of how what might be small innate differences are magnified over time by cultural forces. To put it another way, there's no reason to expect our sons to be any less empathetic than our daughters. Socialization is almost certainly a more potent force than genetics in raising compassionate boys.

Some scholars have also argued that females may develop higher levels of empathy because men hold more status and power than women in almost every culture. Tuning in to emotional cues and becoming skilled at reading others may, for some girls and women, be key to maintaining their social position and perhaps even their safety. There is certainly research support for this hypothesis, such as the finding that women are better than men at detecting anger.

The premise that girls may become emotionally aware in the name of self-protection underscores another key psychological gender difference: Boys are more aggressive than girls.

My work takes me to many schools, and there's little I enjoy more than watching teenagers interact with one another between classes. When the students convene in the hallways during passing periods, a clear gendered behavioral pattern invariably emerges. The girls tend to catch up with their friends by walking together or huddling in deep conversation. The guys, however, connect through physical contact. Especially when I visit all-boys schools, I'm struck by how the students blithely steer and bump into one another and grab at their friends' shoulders and back-packs.

This observable difference is borne out by research studies documenting that by preschool, boys are significantly more likely than girls to engage in rough-and-tumble play. Males remain more physically aggressive than females throughout their lifespan, hitting their peak level right around age fifteen. Given that fifteen-year-old boys are the ones most likely to be rough-housing with friends or to get into fistfights with their adversaries, one could easily assume that rising testosterone levels account for boys' readiness to rumble. While this explanation seems logical, a systematic review of twenty-seven research studies on the topic found no clear link between testosterone levels and physical aggression in teenage boys. Interestingly, one study did find a link between teen boys' testosterone levels and risk taking, but not between their testosterone and *aggressive* risk taking.

If testosterone is not the main culprit, other factors must be responsible for the reality that our sons tend to be so much more physically aggressive than our daughters. From day one, boys are more physically active than girls, which may cause some parents to accept that their sons' physicality will inevitably lead to more aggression. With that assumption in place, they may unwittingly allow boys to cross more physical boundaries. That said, research finds that adults who don't want to raise pugnacious sons don't have to. Boys who are highly empathetic (likely as a result of parental coaching) and closely monitored by their folks tend to be the least aggressive. Just as parents can raise boys to be every bit as empathetic as girls, they can shape how aggressive their sons turn out to be.

We can also approach this from the opposite direction. Instead of wondering why boys are so physically aggressive, we might ask ourselves why girls aren't *more* that way. Here again, socialization plays a major role. Parents are more likely to actively discourage angry or physically aggressive behavior in their daughters than in their sons. And girls' high levels of empathy matter too. Girls may certainly wish to shove, punch, or pinch their peers but find themselves restrained by their heightened awareness of the hurtful impact of such behavior.

While boys outpace girls on *physical* aggression, it's often assumed that girls make up the difference through *relational* aggression—the term used to describe cruel, but indirect, tactics such as spreading rumors or excluding or manipulating others. This assumption, however, turns out to be a myth. Studies repeatedly show that boys and girls are in a dead heat when it comes to their use of relational aggression. Boys are not only more physically aggressive than girls, but they are also just as likely as their female classmates to be unkind in ways that aren't physical.

It may seem counterintuitive that boys use just as much indirect aggression as girls, especially when a term like "mean girls" circulates freely and has no clear male equivalent. And we seem to *hear* about girls hurting their peers' feelings by badmouthing and excluding them more than we hear about boys doing the same.

So how do we explain the fact that girls are perceived as using more relational aggression than boys? Let's look at it through the lens of "boys distract, girls discuss." Consider how two different sixth graders—we'll call them Devon and Avery—might react to being deliberately left out at school. Should Devon discover that he's not welcome at his regular lunch table (perhaps because an unkind classmate started a rumor that Devon is "gross"), there's a decent chance he'll manage this painful situation by "trying to not think about it," as boys often do when they feel uneasy. He might look for another place to sit, or give up on lunch altogether and head to the library to get lost in a book. Though Devon undoubtedly feels terrible, he may keep his feelings entirely to himself, even when he gets home. There he might look for fresh ways to distract himself until the hurt of the day wears off. Likewise, the boys in his class who feel uneasy about the cruel rumor might manage *their* discomfort by changing the subject when the rumor comes up, or by making a dismissive joke about it.

Avery, on the other hand, might react to the same situation quite differently. She could find a compassionate classmate with whom she can speak freely, and perhaps tearfully, about being excluded from her regular table. The classmate, who now likely feels upset on Avery's behalf, may manage *her* discomfort by asking other girls what's going on, thus starting a buzz around the mean rumor and its impact on Avery. After school, Avery might go home and talk with her parents, or perhaps a loving older sister, about her miserable day. Avery's female classmates, for their part, might process the situation by chewing it over with one another, or maybe by sharing it at home with their own parents.

In short, the same unkind event could land with a muted thud among boys, yet create a vast ripple effect among girls. From this angle, it's easy to see how classmates and adults might be much more aware of the relational aggression that takes place among girls, even if, in reality, girls are no meaner in this way.

## Girls and Anger

What about girls and *anger*, which can seem like aggression's first cousin? As every parent of a daughter knows, girls do in fact get mad. Before adolescence, boys consistently express more anger and physical aggression than girls do. But by the teenage years, girls express more anger than teenage boys do, though they continue to lag behind them in physical aggression.

Girls also outmatch boys in the frequency with which they display contempt. Parents of daughters probably aren't surprised to hear this. Girls are often quite comfortable expressing disdain, and will do so verbally—deploying the dismissive terms of the moment such as "basic" or "irrelevant" to brand someone as unoriginal or beneath consideration—or gifting us with a withering facial expression. Our daughters' capacity for derision can be impressive to behold, though it's probably easier for us parents to admire when it's not aimed our way.

However, research demonstrates that girls and women are aware that they are more likely than boys and men to face negative consequences if they let their anger show. Trying to get at the conditions under which young women express anger, an extremely clever study asked male and female university students to participate in what were falsely billed as two unrelated experiments. In the first, the participants were instructed to write an essay about their views on the death penalty. They were told that their essays would be graded by another research participant, and that cash prizes were available for good essays. The study was rigged to provoke anger in half of the participants by giving them low essay grades along with the feedback, allegedly from the grader, that their essays were "naïve" and "immature," regardless of what they actually wrote.

With half of the research participants now hopping mad, the experimenters introduced the second study. This one was allegedly about taste preferences. The research participants were given tortilla chips and spicy hot sauce and asked to decide how much hot sauce their partner in this new study would be required to consume. In an unexpected twist—that was wholly fabricated by the experimenters—the participants were told that "by the luck of the draw" their partner in this second experiment just happened to be the same person who graded their essay in the first experiment! The researchers added one *more* twist before handing over the hot sauce: Half of the participants were told that they'd meet their partner when the experiment ended, and half were told that they would not.

What did the study find? Both the male and female participants reported feeling similar levels of anger. Further, compared to the people who got good grades on their essays, the research participants who got bad grades were heavy-handed with the hot sauce (the study's measure of the expression of anger). Perhaps most interesting, the angry guys in the study gave the same dose of hot sauce to their research partners regardless of whether they thought they would soon be meeting. In contrast, the angry young women gave less hot sauce when they were told they'd have to meet their research partners, but more—in an amount matching that of the guys—when told they *wouldn't* be meeting their research partner.

In the end, the participants never had to meet their research partner, because, as the experimenters ultimately explained to the participants, no such partner ever existed. But the study's clever methodology demonstrated an important point: Girls and women know that they are likely to pay a higher social price for getting mad, and they reserve their anger for situations where they can safely express it.

To be sure, the risks of expressing anger are even more of an issue for girls who are subject to the added pressures of racism. When Black girls get mad, they are often met with a disproportionately harsh disciplinary response. Compared to white girls, Black girls are more likely to be punished at school for "talking back" or being "unladylike," and to be arrested for acting in ways that are considered to be "disrespectful."

## Gender and the Adultification of Black Teens

The markedly punitive response to Black girls' anger is hardly the only example of racism shaping the emotional lives of Black teenagers. Survey research (which tends to draw on predominantly white respondents) demonstrates that Black children and adolescents are subject to *adultification*—they are seen as older than they actually are. Compared to their white counterparts of the same age, Black girls are generally viewed as being less in need of protection, nurturing, comfort, or support and Black boys are generally viewed as being less endowed with childlike innocence and more deserving of blame.

With adultification comes a racist amplification of gendered stereotypes. Numerous studies show that, compared to white peers, Black girls are widely perceived as more sexual and Black boys are widely perceived as more dangerous.

What does this mean for the day-to-day lives of Black adolescent girls? In many schools, they are more likely to be sexually harassed than girls who are white. Further, research demonstrates that their complaints about harassment tend to be ignored or minimized by school personnel. Studies of how Black girls experience their school days reveal, unsurprisingly and sadly, a sense of feeling both physically and emotionally unsafe around their male peers and invisible to—or held responsible by—the adults they are hoping will step in to protect them.

For Black boys, adultification and the heightened gendered stereotypes that come with it mean that they are viewed by much of the world through hostility-colored glasses. In a study that starkly demonstrated this point, researchers showed a predominantly white group of college students video vignettes of elementary-school-aged actors engaging in behavior that could be interpreted as aggressive, such as stepping on another child's homework while running by, walking away with another child's video game, or throwing away another child's work while clean-ing up a classroom. Half of the young male actors were Black and the other half were white. After watching the vignettes, the re-search participants rated how hostile they believed the behaviors to be. Black boys were rated as being more aggressive than the white boys in every single video vignette, despite engaging in the exact same behavior. The stereotype of Black boys as hostile or aggressive gains strength as they get older. Other research has found that every additional year of perceived age (which for Black boys is already likely to be higher than their actual age) increases the odds that Black boys, but not white boys, will be viewed as hostile.

For Black teenage boys, this means that they are overdisci-plined at school. They are also disproportionately subjected by law enforcement authorities to racial profiling, arrest, detention, prosecution, and lethal force. It also means that many Black fam-ilies endure the stomach-turning rite of passage of having "The Talk" with their sons—and, often, daughters—sometimes long before they become teenagers. In an effort to proactively prepare their children for encounters with police or other adults in posi-tions of authority, "The Talk" typically details the heightened risks faced by Black teens even when they are engaged in ordinary activities, like driving or walking down the street with a group of friends. It centers on advising young people on how they can try to maintain their safety in interactions with police and other au-thority figures, such as by keeping their hands visible, remaining calm, being polite, and answering all questions asked.

The Recommended Resources list at the back of this book in-cludes texts that may be of particular support to adults raising or caring for Black teenagers. I cannot, as a white person raising white teenagers, fathom the emotional complexities of partici-pating on either side of conversations such as "The Talk." I can, however, as a psychologist, lament the grave and exceptional burden borne by Black adolescents as they strive to grow into adult-hood.

## Gender Differences in Psychopathology

Let's review what we've established so far. From day one, children are socialized down two different psychological paths. We allow girls to express sadness and fear, tend to discourage their anger, and cultivate their ability to talk about feelings when they are upset. We teach boys to suppress feelings of vulnerability, expect them to be aggressive, and, when they're distressed, encourage them to use distraction or to find other ways to tough it out.

This emotional typecasting underlies and helps explain stark gender differences in the psychological disorders we see among teenagers. When adolescent emotional difficulties become so intense or pervasive that they warrant professional intervention, two clear gendered diagnostic categories emerge.

Girls are far more likely than boys to be diagnosed with what we call *internalizing disorders,* namely anxiety and depression. Boys are far more likely than girls to be diagnosed with *externalizing disorders,* such as oppositional defiant disorder or conduct disorder (the first describes persistently angry behavior, the second chronic delinquency). To put it another way, when in emotional pain, girls tend to collapse in on themselves and become anxious, numb, or sad, while boys tend to lash out and often get themselves in trouble.

One way to understand this split is to see it as the extreme outcome of the gendered rules for emotional expression. Because we expect and accept that girls will feel sadness and anxiety, those emotions often become the modes by which all of their psychological distress is expressed, including anger if there is no safe way to express it. How does this happen? The defense mechanism of turning an unacceptable emotion *back against the self* explains this dynamic. For example, a girl who feels that a parent, teacher, or classmate is terrible may worry that expressing such a feeling outwardly will come at too high a cost. Instead, she may reroute it into the depressing or worrisome belief that *she*, in fact, is the terrible one.

As for boys, we expect that they will be more aggressive than girls, so anger becomes the "acceptable" mode by which their painful feelings can find relief. A boy who is deeply sad or severely anxious needs an outlet for his distress, and if he doesn't feel that he has permission to let people know he's hurting, it's a good bet that he will discharge his unwanted emotions by acting out. I watched this painful dynamic at work when, in my midtwenties, I was working as a full-time staff member at a residential psychiatric facility, where I was assigned to a unit for adolescent boys. All of the boys in my care came from extremely difficult and disrupted family situations, which went a long way toward explaining why they suffered from emotional challenges severe enough to require inpatient treatment. While they were physically aggressive quite often, they were all but guaranteed to be so right after a planned visit from a parent or guardian. Before and during these visits, the boys were usually especially well behaved, because, it always seemed to me, they were full of hope that the visit would be warmer, kinder, more loving, or less chaotic than it typically turned out to be. After the visit, the boys were often acutely sad and disappointed. But rather than weeping, which would have been entirely appropriate, they tended to discharge their suffering by antagonizing the other residents and looking for a fight.

If you have concerns that your teen may be struggling with depression or anxiety, consult a health professional for guidance. If your teen constantly breaks rules, argues all the time, or harms animals, people, or property, don't assume that punishment is your best or only option. One of the cardinal rules in psychology is that teenagers act awful when they feel awful. Teens lash out when they're in pain, and they deserve our compassion and access to therapeutic interventions when they do.

## Helping Girls Handle Anger

The extremes of internalizing and externalizing disorders represent the endpoints of two roads we don't want our teenagers going down. Teenagers of all genders should be able to express the full range of emotions; we want them to have the right feelings at the right time—regardless of the gender rules—and to learn how to manage those emotions effectively.

For our sons, this will largely mean helping them get comfortable with expressing sadness, fear, worry, and other emotions that might leave them feeling vulnerable. For our daughters, this will mean helping them know what to do with their anger.

Odds are that you'll have plenty of opportunities to help your daughter make best use of her temper, because home is probably where she's most likely to express it. Though your daughter's stormy moods might unsettle your otherwise peaceful household, take comfort in the knowledge that she feels safe expressing her annoyance at home. And when your girl is mad but civil, go ahead and engage with her about what's wrong, even if you're the one she's mad at. There are two reasons for this. First, if we want her to take her own emotions seriously, we need to do the same. Second, we want to reinforce her right to express her anger by giving it our attention.

It may also be the case that your daughter is unfailingly charming elsewhere but serves up extra-spicy hostility at home. Friends of mine with sons have registered shock at what they hear from parents of daughters about what girls say at home in the heat of anger. Boys, they've remarked, just get mad. Girls sometimes say things that are meant to cut deep.

When any teen says something that is cruel or mean, it's time to do some teaching. What's the lesson? That their anger isn't the problem, but the way they are showing it is. When your teenager goes too far, you can respond calmly with "I don't think that's how you meant for that to come out. Try again?" or "You might be mad, but you can't talk to me that way," or "You may well have a point but you need to find a civil way to express it," or "I don't speak to you that way. You may not speak to me that way." Adolescents often realize that what they've said is over the line as soon as they hear their own words out loud. A calm, firm redirection can get things back on track quickly and help avert a blowup.

When Black girls assert themselves because they are angry, or simply to stand up for themselves, we need to take seriously the fact that they are often the victims of a punitive racial bias. Indeed, research finds that in K–12 public schools, Black girls are six times more likely to be suspended than white girls even though they defy behavioral expectations at the same rate. Any question of whether a Black girl's anger is being appropriately expressed needs to come second to the question of whether she is being held to stricter standards than her white peers.

Finally, feel free to marvel at how teens of any color find ways to thread the needle of needing to express anger without getting themselves in trouble. I think here of a clever and strong-minded twelve-year-old girl I cared for in my practice. After describing her condescending and dictatorial social studies teacher in great detail, she told me, "When I can't take it anymore, I shove my hands in my pockets and give him the finger."

## Helping Boys Talk About Their Feelings

When the COVID-19 pandemic turned everyone's life upside down, I had to suspend my usual travel to speak at schools about topics related to youth mental health and adolescent development. But educators knew how painful it was for their students to endure the isolation, stress, and anxiety (and sometimes trauma and bereavement) caused by the pandemic. To offer support, a number of middle and high schools invited me to meet with groups of their students over Zoom.

Before long, I struck upon an approach that worked well and opened up a whole new vista on teenagers' emotional lives. I began my meetings with the students (sometimes two or three hundred at a time) with a twenty-minute explanation of the psychological science of stress and anxiety. I talked them through strategies to buffer their worries and fears and described ways they could protect their mental health while living under extraordinarily difficult conditions. After covering these central topics and, perhaps most important, giving the students a sense of how I empathized with what they were going through, I then invited them to use the chat feature to "ask me anything."

In advance of these meetings, I worked with each school to set up the chat so that students' messages would be seen only by me. When it was time for them to ask me their questions, I explained that I would read each question aloud before answering it but would not read out who had asked it. This routine made for remarkable conversations. The chats filled quickly with specific inquiries about personal subjects. I took the questions one by one and did my best to repay each student's trust in me by offering answers that were direct and, I hoped, useful. Almost immediately, a clear pattern emerged. The girls were active in the chat, but I often got the impression that they were running by me questions that they were also discussing with others. They asked how to balance the demands of school with other obligations, what my views on psychiatric medications were, how to best support a fragile friend, and so on. The boys, however, poured their hearts out.

They filled the chat with topics that they didn't seem to be sharing with anyone else. "How can you tell if a girl likes you?" and "I think I might be gay and am afraid to tell anyone" and "My parents fight all the time and I cry myself to sleep at night and don't know what to do." On a few occasions boys even commented in the chat, "We should do meetings like this all the time—even after the pandemic—I would *never* ask questions like this in front of my classmates!"

The safety of the Zoom space revealed what many parents know: Boys have deep feelings and long for intimate connections with others. And indeed, despite cultural pressures to harden themselves, boys *do* find ways to share closely held emotions. Some guys feel comfortable expressing worry, sadness, and fear at home, or with like-minded male or female peers with whom they develop close and powerful friendships. Others seek out romantic relationships because they yearn for emotional connection at least as much as they crave physical intimacy.

Given that boys *do* want to talk about their inner worlds, how can we create conditions that foster their ability and willingness to share what's really on their minds? We need to build it into their day. For example, here's a corny but effective strategy: Consider making it a practice to share "roses and thorns" at every family dinner. To do this, each family member describes the best and worst thing that happened that day, with the option of "passing" from time to time when they're not in the mood to share. This simple approach normalizes the idea that everyone runs into situations that leave them feeling scared, frustrated, sad, and anxious. It also allows you to show your teenager how to talk openly about hard things by doing so yourself. When teens find the exercise mortifying, we can go ahead and acknowledge that it's a gimmick while letting them know that we expect their participation anyway.

Building the discussion of painful topics into the routines of family life matters because we know that what gets modeled at home makes a real difference. One research study found that Latino boys are more likely than their white, Black, or Chinese American peers to remain at ease with emotional intimacy late into adolescence. Most of the Latino boys in the study were first- or second-generation immigrants from Puerto Rico or the Dominican Republic who, the researcher surmised, may have enjoyed the protection of belonging to cultures that value emotional expression and interdependence in males and females alike.

If we really want boys to get comfortable talking about their feelings, the men in their lives should not leave the emotional work to women. As one might expect, research shows mothers are more likely than fathers to talk with their children about their inner lives, a finding that makes sense given that we socialize girls and women to be especially fluent in the language of emotion. Kids come to expect that when they bring a personal problem to their dad, they'll get suggestions about how to fix it, but if they bring it to their mom, they'll be helped to talk about how the problem makes them feel. Unfortunately, this only reinforces the idea that discussing feelings is an inherently feminine act.

To counter this preconception, adult men need to make a point of asking boys about what's going on inside and engaging in meaningful conversations about emotions. Instead of offering solutions to boys' problems, they should treat the act of sharing painful experiences with a trustworthy person as a solution unto itself. Which it is. By normalizing the act of talking about feelings, men help boys to view themselves as nuanced and multifaceted and send the message that discussing emotions is just part of what boys and men should do.

In addition to modeling and encouraging the expression of uncomfortable feelings, adults should watch for distress that comes out sideways. Boys who feel that it's their job to be emotionally hardened will sometimes let us know that they are in emotional pain by complaining of headaches or stomachaches. At other times they'll express upset feelings by becoming physically agitated or by being aggressive with their peers or siblings.

If you suspect that uneasy feelings may be driving what you're seeing, check in. Ask with compassion, "Do you think your stomach might be hurting because something's making you feel nervous?" or "It's not like you to go after your brother like that. What's going on?" See if you can get a conversation going about the fact that the boy who is acting out might need to get some feelings off his chest.

If we really want boys to express sadness, fear, apprehension, or any other emotion that might leave them feeling exposed, they need to see that the adult men in their lives are doing the same, be it their own father or any other men they respect. One of my dear female friends has three teenage sons and a large extended family that gets together often. My friend's father, the family patriarch, tears up regularly and unselfconsciously at family celebrations. When her teenage boys affectionately joke, "Look, Grandpa's crying," my friend enthusiastically retorts, "Yes, he is! And you should be crying too!"

## How Peers Reinforce Gender Rules

## (and What to Do About It)

Becoming a teenager means spending more and more time with your peer group, and especially in late middle and early high school, kids hang out mostly with same-sex friends. It has long been observed that the gendered divergence in emotional expression intensifies during adolescence: Girls become more inclined to talk about their feelings, while boys become more prone to managing emotional pain by closing down and relying only on themselves. This is in large part an effect of spending more time with same-sex peers who enforce—and amplify—gendered norms for dealing with emotions.

Among girls, this can take the form of spending *too much* time talking about feelings. Of course, there's a lot to be said for the fact that girls tend to be comfortable turning to their friends for support. And while talking about painful feelings can provide needed relief, it can also tip over into rumination, especially for girls. This is a problem. We define *rumination* as thinking constantly, repetitively, and fruitlessly about a painful subject. It's the psychological equivalent of picking at a wound.

A robust body of research shows that our daughters are more likely to ruminate than our sons, and to have female friends who are willing to engage with them in what we call *co-rumination*—the meticulous and well-meaning group analysis of an emotional injury. Perhaps most concerning, ruminative thinking has been found to contribute to the onset of mood and anxiety disorders in teenagers. When young people deal with difficulties by obsessing, they increase their likelihood of developing depression and anxiety.

Just as constantly dwelling on uncomfortable feelings can make matters worse, refusing to acknowledge emotional vulnerability causes problems, too. Unfortunately for our sons, boys energetically enforce with one another a gendered emotional code that is easily summed up in a single rule: Don't show weakness. By first or second grade, some boys start to accuse their peers of being "crybabies" if they become openly distraught or let on that they feel hurt.

Not long after that, boys begin to aspire to a very narrowly defined version of masculinity that eschews anything that could be considered feminine. Middle and high school boys are well aware that the display of emotional or physical pain will likely be met with accusations of acting "like a girl," or with sexist and homophobic slurs along the lines of being a "pussy" or "homo." Studies of how adolescent boys connect with one another paint a picture of interactions centered on teasing, mocking, and shoving that reinforce a knuckle-dragging version of masculinity and leave no room for emotional vulnerability.

Perhaps the starkest difference in the gendered emotional rules for girls and boys comes up around the universal act of crying. Girls typically feel that they can weep when they need to, and they will do so with little or no embarrassment in the company of friends, parents, siblings, and adults they trust at school. For boys, crying quickly becomes taboo. Though kindergarten boys may not be able to stop themselves from crying at school, adolescent boys have shared with me that they remember feeling acute shame about crying even then. By late elementary school, most boys have figured out how to suppress the impulse to cry and otherwise hide their tender side. In adolescence, crying might at times be allowable among boys, but only under the strictest conditions. As one high school senior explained to me, crying was okay among boys only in situations that were "really big" and communal, such as among the players of a team that had just lost a season-ending game, or if grieving over the death of a classmate.

So, adolescents can push their peers to unhealthy extremes in the management of emotions by talking about feelings either too much or not nearly enough. We should keep an eye out for this in terms of our own interactions with our teenagers and in what we can pick up about their relationships with their friends. When needed, we can work to compensate for these detrimental emotional management styles at home.

With regard to rumination, you've got nothing to worry about if your teenager feels better after putting painful feelings into words. But if you get the sense that continuing to discuss a problem—either with you or with peers—seems only to be aggravating an emotional wound, it's time to step in. When teenagers start spinning their psychological wheels, adults can be most helpful when we encourage them to take another tack. This can be a conversation that begins something like "I'm glad you're talking about what's bothering you because that often helps you feel better. But let's come up with some other options, too. Because sometimes talking about a problem works, and sometimes it seems to leave you feeling worse."

Adolescents are often tremendously supportive of one another. This is wonderful and admirable, but it can also lead to teenagers staying up late into the night, sacrificing their own schoolwork and sleep, to talk or text with a friend who is suffering. If you know or start to suspect that this is happening in your own home, you're right to intervene. Begin by acknowledging how much you respect your teenager's generous devotion, but teach this rule: Friends don't let friends co-ruminate. Ask your teenager to consider the possibility that being always ready and willing to talk about the friend's troubles may be keeping the problem alive or keeping the friend from either putting it behind them or seeking professional help.

If your teenager agrees that a friend seems to be stuck in a ruminating rut, encourage your teen to offer happy distractions as an alternate way to lend support. "I don't know why that girl is ghosting you," your teen might say to the friend, "but if it would help you feel better, we could go thrifting this weekend." If you think the friend needs professional help, not just peer support, you can say to your teen, "You're amazing, but if I broke my leg, I wouldn't ask you to set it. You and I both know that your friend probably deserves the support of a pro. Can I help you figure out how to have that conversation?"

If, as sometimes happens, the friend already has a therapist but continues to lean heavily on your teen for advice, provide coaching along these lines: "It's good for you to be supportive of your friend as she works through her depression. But if you're feeling helpless or overwhelmed, ask her if she's telling her therapist everything she's telling you." As much as teens want to be available for one another, they also recognize that setting appropriate boundaries is often an important part of caring for a friend who is struggling.

While girls, in particular, may need help setting boundaries with friends who share too much, boys, for their part, often have the opposite problem. Adults need to address the fact that boys encourage one another to adopt emotional self-reliance and stoicism as defining features of their emerging masculinity. A friend of mine who is the mother of a fifth grader found a great opening for this conversation when her son mentioned that one of his classmates had burst into tears at recess. She started by asking her thoughtful, emotionally attuned boy what he made of the situation (he felt awful for the kid), and then spun that off into a deeper exploration of *why* he felt so bad for his classmate.

Her son, it turned out, was more concerned that the tears were "embarrassing" for his classmate than he was about whatever caused the tears in the first place. Without expecting any response, she took the opportunity to let her son know that she was really sorry that boys weren't allowed to show hurt feelings at school, because they have as much of a right to express pain and receive support as girls do. In truth, telling our sons that boys shouldn't feel ashamed to reveal fear, sadness, pain, or anxiety in front of their peers will not, in all likelihood, put them at ease with actually doing it. They are acutely aware of the risks of acting "like a girl" and may be understandably reluctant to let down their guard. But it's still worth making the point that exposing vulnerability isn't the problem; the rules against it are.

Keep your ears open for moments when your son might—even jokingly—remark that another boy is being a "wuss," a "mama's boy," or some other slur along those lines. Or look for instances in TV shows or movies where boys or men ridicule one another for expressing "weak" emotions. When these examples come your way, chime in with something like, "I think you know this, but I'm going to say it anyway: It's wrong to make fun of a guy for getting upset. You are never to do it. And if you see someone else giving a hurting kid a hard time, you need to be good to the kid who's hurting, tell the other kid to knock it off, or both."

If you try this at home, don't be surprised if your teen responds with a shrug or an eye roll. No self-respecting adolescent will reply to such guidance with "I'm so glad that you brought this up and I really appreciate your suggestions." This isn't a problem so long as we remember that our goal isn't to put an end to macho nonsense everywhere, but to make sure that our sons have our voice in their head when they see it or think about joining in. Adolescents can signal indifference to our advice and still take in what we've said. As the mother of two teenagers, I find that it works best for all involved if I receive their shrugs or eye rolls as a nonverbal way of saying "I heard you."

## The Roots of Harassment

By the time they are teenagers, our sons and daughters tend to occupy two very different emotional worlds. Girls get to be whole. Boys have to be tough. By adolescence, girls drive along a broad emotional highway, while our teenage sons restrict themselves to an increasingly narrow lane. As boys move into manhood they face ongoing pressures to cloak any emotion that could be characterized as feminine or "weak," and some start proving their manliness by belittling girls and women. For the many social benefits that come with being male, it's easy to overlook how boys are hemmed in by gendered expectations around emotions. While our daughters have it better than our sons when it comes to the free expression of their feelings, both boys and girls pay a price for the fact that our sons grow up in a culture that can leave them at a loss when they feel hurt or insecure.

Several years ago, I spent a day giving talks at a private co-ed PK–12 school in Pennsylvania. Between my afternoon meeting with the faculty and my evening presentation for the parents, I caught an early dinner with a middle school teacher, the high school principal, and the school librarian. Eventually, the conversation turned to a recent incident that had understandably troubled many of the students and adults at the school. The librarian had discovered that a handful of high school boys were circulating a digital document in which they ranked their female classmates in terms of "ho-ness," "hotness," and "fuckability."

The principal shared that in addition to disciplining the participating boys, he was now looking for a good antiharassment program to add to the high school curriculum.

"What they did was beyond the pale," he said, "yet it didn't strike them, or most of their classmates, as a big deal at all." He was eager to find a way to shift the norms around misogynist behavior, yet realized that it might be impossible to prevent future incidents like this one. All the same, he added, "We have to try to find a way to challenge a school culture that seems to be comfortable with unbelievably degrading behavior."

I told him that I couldn't agree more, but that I thought high school was too late to start addressing the problem.

"Boys are harassing girls by sixth grade," I said, "if not earlier." The middle school teacher nodded in agreement. "If you want to prevent this kind of degrading behavior, you need to take it on starting in fifth grade at the latest. And honestly, we need to help parents start earlier than that. So long as boys don't know how to handle feeling insecure, they're going to start demeaning girls by age eleven or sooner."

When tween boys start to mistreat girls, we often blame their behavior on sexist content in the movies, television, video games, or online media they consume. These influences may well be a factor, but there's another reason that we tend to overlook: In middle school boys are suddenly, and seriously, outmatched by their female classmates. This abrupt—and for some boys alarming—development can be explained by the fact that our daughters hit puberty about two years before our sons do. Girls' developmental head start has major physical and cognitive implications.

From ages eleven to thirteen, the average girl is taller than the average boy. And at these ages, many girls can run as fast and jump as high as the guys in their class. Boys can usually throw farther and harder than their female classmates (likely as a result of practice), but if a sixth, seventh, or eighth grade boy challenges a girl to a footrace, there's a good chance he'll lose. For boys who are starting to define masculinity in terms of being big, strong, and—above all—better than girls, the action at recess can be humiliating.

What's happening in the classroom is likely to make matters even worse. Puberty also drives a growth spurt in brain development that puts middle school girls about two years ahead of boys in their intellectual and cognitive functioning. Middle school girls get better grades than boys, as they have since elementary school, and their new mental horsepower also allows them to think in increasingly sophisticated ways. Unless a tween boy has won the developmental lottery of hitting puberty early, it's easy to imagine how hard it might be for him to feel good about himself at school. As one seventh grade boy explained to me, "Among guys, there's nothing worse in the whole world than getting beat by a girl."

Thus middle school boys find themselves caught in a perfect emotional storm. They're getting beaten by girls left and right; many have embraced a notion of masculinity that makes losing to a girl especially humbling; *and* they don't feel safe expressing any feelings of vulnerability. Not all boys will handle this well. Unfortunately, a subset of guys who feel that their formidable female classmates are making them look "weak" will try to manage the situation by taking girls down a few pegs.

Girls can certainly be unkind to one another in middle school, but research shows that boys are their main antagonists. By sixth grade, boys are the ones more likely to tease, scare, or go out of their way to upset the girls in their class. By seventh grade, if not sooner, boys begin to put a sexual spin on their bullying, often by making vulgar jokes, comments, or gestures, and sometimes by physically grabbing female classmates. When this happens, some adults focus on the sexual nature of boys' behavior and dismiss their harassment as a clumsy or misguided form of flirtation. This is a mistake. Sexual harassment is about power at any age. Boys who treat girls in degrading ways are abusing their cultural power to try to elevate themselves and ease their own insecurities. In fact, research shows that when boys bully girls, it's likely to be the least popular boys in a class mistreating the most popular girls.

This is a terrible situation for everyone involved. It's not good for a boy to try to maintain his self-esteem by belittling girls. It's even worse if he discovers that he *does* feel bigger when he makes girls feel small. Now the groundwork is laid for the young man to seek self-worth through aggressive, sexist behavior. In sum, he's headed down the last path we would want our sons to take.

And of course it's not good for girls to be on the receiving end of boys' mistreatment. As one would expect, girls experience a significant amount of psychological distress as a result of being sexually harassed, and such harassment likely contributes to the alarming, well-documented drop-off in self-esteem among adolescent girls.

## Teens and Self-Esteem

So how do we help our tweens and teens feel good about themselves through middle school? We don't want our sons to torment girls because they're feeling insecure, and we don't want our daughters to lose confidence as a result of being harassed by boys. The best bet? Helping all teenagers develop a sturdy sense of self-worth.

The idea of cultivating self-esteem in children has a checkered past. It has been associated with giving awards to everyone for everything and bathing kids in empty affirmations. That's not what we're talking about here. A true sense of self-worth does not come from telling our children that they are special or important. Rather, teenagers feel good about themselves for well-earned accomplishments and meaningful contributions.

Some tweens and teens thrive academically, athletically, artistically, in extracurricular activities, or at their jobs. But not all adolescents shine in conventional settings, and even the ones who do will have days where things don't go well. Accordingly, every young person should have ways to feel good about themselves that they are able to control.

One reliable way to ensure self-esteem is to be of service to others. For tweens and teens, this can range from caring for younger siblings or pets, to having chores that make a real contribution to the household, to participating in regular volunteer work in the broader community. Self-worth can be fragile in young people. When a star athlete has a terrible game, or a strong student fails a test, it's easy for them to feel like the bottom of a shoe. But when our kids make themselves useful, two good things happen at once. First, their attention is pulled outward and they get a break from worrying about their own concerns and shortcomings. Second, they are reminded of all that they have to offer. As people sometimes say, it's hard to be sad and useful at the same time.

In addition to being of service, tweens and teenagers also benefit when they have time for pursuits that are meaningful and important to them and are not done for the sake of a grade, or credit, or their college applications. I've seen adolescents get serious about knitting, juggling, cooking, and square dancing. I know a teenage violinist who played with a local youth orchestra but was proudest of her ability to figure out how to play pop songs just for herself. Young people seem to develop an especially sturdy form of self-esteem when they refine a skill or a craft that they choose to pursue on their own and not, as so often happens, because they are told or expected to do so.

There will still be times, however, when our kids feel unhappy about how they stack up against their peers or wish that their abilities would develop more quickly. In these moments, it can be especially useful to remind young people that getting good at something may take time, and that effort and persistence will help get them where they want to go.

To protect self-worth in middle school, we should work to help our children have reliable sources of self-esteem in place by the late elementary grades. When boys feel good about ways in which they are useful and take pleasure in cultivating interests and abilities, it's easier for them to weather the interval when it will be hard to keep up with the girls at school. Girls, for their part, need to have dependable sources of self-esteem for when they arrive at puberty and are faced with a host of new challenges. In addition to often being harassed by boys at school, girls can't help but become aware of broader cultural pressures having to do with their appearance and attractiveness. Girls who can point to their meaningful contributions and burgeoning skills have reliable ways to feel good about themselves as they move into adolescence, when, inevitably, they will run into feedback suggesting that their containers are a lot more important than their contents.

As for harassment, keep an eye on how your son is coming to define masculinity and talk with him in specific terms about what it means to be manly. Make it clear that "real men" have no need to tease, pressure, degrade, or demean others. Instead, they take pride in being decent, respectful, considerate, and quick to defend anyone who is being mistreated. For *all* of our teenagers, we should initiate a conversation about sexual harassment by sixth grade or sooner. Consider saying something like "I hate to say this, but before too long, some kids may start giving other kids a hard time about their bodies, or making them feel uncomfortable by saying sexual things. If it happens to you or a friend, let me know. That behavior is totally out of line and I'm here to help." When teens share news of harassment, figure out how best to alert the school and hold it to the expectation that sexual harassment will be treated as the bullying behavior that it is.

## Beyond the Traditional Gender Binary

Over the last ten years there has been a dramatic shift in the expression and acceptance of nontraditional gender identities among teenagers. In many communities, it's no longer unusual for teens to identify as gender-fluid, gender nonbinary, genderless, or transgender—a group of gender identities that, at the time of this writing, is often referred to as *gender-expansive*. Many adults may be scrambling to catch up to this cultural quantum leap, but young people tend to greet the changing view of traditional gender norms as unremarkable and long overdue.

If you are the parent of a gender-questioning or gender-expansive teen, no matter your own views on their nontraditional gender status, your first job is to protect your child's mental and physical health. Despite growing acceptance, teens who do not fit within traditional gender categories still find themselves in a difficult position. They may feel the need to sacrifice what they know to be true about themselves in order to conform to long-standing gender norms, or they may express themselves authentically and face the questioning, stigmatization, discrimination, hostility, and even risk of physical violence that can come with doing so. Or they may find themselves in an extended state of uncertainty and need to simultaneously juggle both their own and other people's questions about their identity. Given what they are up against, these teens often suffer, and as a result, they have higher rates of substance use, depression, anxiety, and suicidal thoughts and behaviors than their gender-conventional peers.

If a teenager is in need of professional support, as many adolescents expressing a nontraditional gender identity understandably are, parents can work to connect them with seasoned and sensitive clinicians. Should teenagers express an interest in biological interventions—such as taking medications to suppress puberty, undergoing cross-sex hormone treatment, or having gender-affirming surgical procedures—families do not have to weigh these complex decisions alone. Many communities have university-affiliated clinics with departments that specialize in caring for gender-expansive teenagers. These departments rely on multidisciplinary teams made up of physicians, mental health professionals, and gender specialists who attend to teens' safety and well-being while adhering to research-based approaches to care. Parents should not hesitate to draw on the experience and wisdom of these professionals should challenging questions arise.

Your second job is to protect your working relationship with your teenager. The best approach is to treat your teenager as the driver of their own gender car, with parents viewing yourselves as loving front-seat passengers who are along for the ride. Teens may or may not know where they are ultimately headed, gender-wise; and as their parents, we cannot know or control where they'll end up. But we do have a great deal of say over how they feel about themselves and their relationship with us during the journey.

So how do we maintain a healthy relationship with a gender-questioning or -expansive teenager? For starters, by not confusing gender identity with sexual orientation. People sometimes wrongly conflate expressing a nontraditional gender identity with coming out as gay or lesbian, bisexual, or pansexual (attracted to all genders). In fact, gender identity and sexual orientation operate independently of each other. To put it another way, the gender that people feel themselves to be is unrelated to whom they find sexually attractive. When teens express a nontraditional gender identity, remember that they are sharing information about who they are, not about whom they are drawn to romantically.

Next, don't tell them that they are just "going through a

phase." In truth, gender identity tends to evolve over time for everyone. A middle-aged woman or man probably doesn't think about what it means to be feminine or masculine the same way they did when they were younger. But how, when, or whether gender identity evolves is entirely personal and can't be known from the outside. Telling teenagers that they'll outgrow their gender-questioning or -expansive identities will almost certainly be received as invalidating, hurtful, and rejecting.

Instead, parents will want to respond empathetically, not react abruptly, to the news of a teen's nontraditional gender identity, such as by saying, "I'm so glad you felt you could tell me." If, however, you are caught off guard, saying "What you are sharing is big and important. You're probably not surprised that I need some time to take it in" is better than "Where is this coming from?" Similarly, responding with "I care about you so much and worry that you'll be mistreated by others" is better than "What will people think?" And sharing that "We love *you*, not your gender" is better than "But you've always been my *son*." Parents who have had a knee-jerk reaction or realize in retrospect that they have said something they regret can and should try to make it right. Here are some words with which to start: "I realize now that I responded in a way that must have hurt you. I needed some time to think about what you said; it was a lot to take in. I'm sorry and am asking for your forgiveness."

This is not to say that parents won't have their own doubts, worries, fears, and misgivings about their teen's nontraditional gender identity. They may feel anxious about their child's future and safety, may struggle with not knowing what might be ahead on their child's gender journey, and may wonder what "caused" their teenager's nontraditional identity. Parents can sometimes mourn the loss of long-anticipated gendered conventions—such as walking their daughter down the aisle at her wedding—and may also need to reconcile their love for their child with their own previously held assumptions, or with their religious or cultural beliefs.

If your child's gender identity strains your relationship with them, seek counseling from a family therapist who can help you protect your child's all-important mental health and relationship with you. Research finds that teenagers who feel that their parents support and affirm their nontraditional gender identity have vastly better mental health outcomes than those who feel unsupported or rejected at home. Parents may also want to seek professional support for themselves, as those who have a place to process their own feelings about their teen's nontraditional gender identity are often better able to maintain their bond with their teenager at home.

For teens, society's gender rules can be a significant barrier to being in touch with their own emotions or managing their feelings effectively. As parents, we need to push against cultural expectations that seek to limit what our sons and daughters are "supposed" to feel and what they are allowed to express. Our goal, of course, is to help our teens embrace the full range of their emotional experiences—and given that they are teenagers, those moods are complex. So let's turn our attention to making sense of the emotional upheaval that is entirely natural to adolescence.

■ ■ ■ ■ ■

## CHAPTER THREE

# Seismic Shift: How Adolescence Puts a New Emotional Spin on Everyday Life

On a weekday in January, I met my friend Valerie for lunch at our favorite local restaurant. It's a place with big windows, a friendly staff, and a chicken curry wrap that always hits the spot. We were still taking off our heavy winter coats when Valerie jumped right in.

"I almost texted you over the holidays—but didn't want to bug you around Christmas. Things got pretty intense at our house."

"Well, you know you can always reach out . . . but what happened?" I asked. "Is everyone okay?"

"Yeah, things seem okay now. Honestly, though . . . Nat was a total wreck over the break."

Nat—Natalie—is Valerie's daughter, who had just turned thirteen. I had known Nat since she was in preschool and had always thought of her as one of those kids for whom still waters ran deep. She was sweet, introverted, and wonderfully creative. An accomplished artist, she liked to think up fantastical creatures and then bring them to life in detailed colored-pencil drawings. Given what I knew about Nat, I didn't expect to hear her mom describe her as a "total wreck."

"It started on Christmas Day," said Valerie. "After opening presents at our house, we went over to my parents' place, where we exchanged gifts with my folks and my sister's family." Valerie explained that Nat's grandparents usually give her clothes for Christmas, gladly taking direction from Valerie about what Nat might want.

"They got her a really cute sweatshirt and a jean jacket—but I could see right away that she was disappointed, like, *really* disappointed. Nat held it together while we were there, but she fell apart the minute we got in the car."

Valerie explained that Nat had started weeping on the way home and continued to cry off and on for the rest of the day.

"She didn't like the clothes they had picked out—but that wasn't the real problem. The issue was that she was mad at herself for not appreciating what they had given her. Then, on top of that, she became upset with herself for the fact that she was so upset! Honestly, it was awful. Nothing we did or said seemed to help, and Nat was as weirded out by her meltdown as we were. At one point she stood doubled over sobbing in the living room. Between sobs she kept saying that she didn't understand why she was falling apart, or why she couldn't pull it together."

"How long did this last?" I asked tenderly.

"She calmed down by dinnertime, and things were pretty normal for about a week."

"Then what happened?"

"We had a plan to take down the Christmas tree and the decorations the last Sunday of break as we usually do. We put on holiday music and everyone helps and it's always a really good time. Out of nowhere, Nat fell apart again. She started weeping, and this time the problem was that she didn't want Christmas to be over. The hardest part—and this is why I almost called you— was that she kept saying that she felt 'like a crazy person.' She knew that putting away Christmas wasn't that big a deal, but she couldn't stop crying."

"I feel so bad for her," I said. "It's awful to become undone like that, and even worse for kids when they can't make sense of what's happening. Here's what I can tell you—and this is something that you might want to share with Nat: Her holiday meltdown was the product of her newly gawky brain."

## A Brain Under Major Construction

Psychologists divide child and adolescent development into three broad stages. The first stage, early childhood, runs from birth to age five, and it's characterized by a great deal of emotional intensity, as those who have parented through it know well. Babies cry, toddlers tantrum, and preschoolers are always ripe for a power struggle. Early childhood is then followed by a stage we call *latency*, which runs from ages six to ten. In this phase, supercharged emotions are, as the name of the stage implies, in hibernation. Latency-age kids tend to be balanced, easygoing, and a lot of fun to parent. They sometimes get very excited or very upset, but they can generally manage their feelings pretty effectively, either on their own or with our support. Then, around age ten or eleven, as latency gives way to adolescence, the potent emotions that had been lying quiet suddenly come roaring back to the scene.

"Wait," you might be thinking, "are you really saying that adolescence begins at *eleven*?" Indeed, the word "teenager" suggests that we shouldn't expect teen behavior until around age thirteen, so many parents are taken aback when their fifth or sixth grader suddenly quits cuddling, wishes for more privacy, and bristles at being called a "cutie patootie" or any other previously acceptable term of affection. But psychologists mark the beginning of adolescence at age ten or eleven, because puberty is already under way for many girls and boys by then. And even before the outward physical signs of puberty become apparent, the adolescent brain is starting to undergo a major physiological renovation.

If adolescence starts at age ten or eleven, you may be wondering when it ends. The answer depends on what aspect of adolescence we're measuring. If we're focusing on when young people usually become mostly independent and self-sufficient, we'd probably mark the end of adolescence somewhere around age nineteen, as the World Health Organization does. But if we're approaching this from the perspective of brain development, we'd say age twenty-four, because that's when the neurological changes that begin during adolescence are finally complete.

Indeed, if we could take a tour inside your teenager's brain, we would find a massive rewiring project at work. Transforming a child brain into an adult one involves adding a huge number of neurons—the highly specialized cells that communicate information throughout the brain and body. Although the brain generates new neurons at every age, teenagers form them at a rate four to five times that of adults. At the very same time the adolescent brain is busily forming new neurons, it's also subtracting underused ones—a process known as "pruning"—at a pace unmatched at any other point in life.

Thinking of neurons as wires that receive and send information helps us to understand another upgrading process that is also taking place in the brain during adolescence: increased *myelination*. Like the colorful plastic coatings that insulate actual wires, myelin is a fatty substance that surrounds individual neurons. The so-called *myelin sheath,* by insulating neurons, speeds the transmission of the electrical impulses that they use to communicate with one another. By the end of adolescence, the brain has been overhauled and upgraded. The combined processes of adding and pruning neurons and enhancing the myelin sheaths make the teenage brain faster, more powerful, and more efficient than it has ever been before.

But parents and teenagers need to know that this major neurological renovation does not proceed evenly throughout the brain. It's first geared toward the lower, evolutionarily ancient regions of the brain and only later toward the higher, more sophisticated ones.

One of the first areas to be upgraded is the *limbic system*. Sitting deep within the brain, it houses the *amygdala,* a structure tasked with evaluating incoming information and generating emotions. Later, the renovation project moves on to the *prefrontal* region of the brain, responsible for planning, decision making, and maintaining a sense of perspective. While a great deal of brain maturation reaches completion during the teenage years, it may not be until age twenty-four, as I mentioned, that this final phase of the transformation is complete.

When I described Nat's brain as "gawky," I was trying to convey the lopsided nature of normal neurological development. At thirteen, the emotion centers of her brain are newly enhanced and thus able to bulldoze the comparatively weak perspective-maintaining centers that are still years away from reaching full maturity. As a result, the uneven neurological development taking place in young teenagers like Nat creates conditions that can readily turn them into emotional "wrecks."

After explaining to Valerie these changes in the teenage brain, I offered reassurance. "The good news," I said, "is that the overall force of Nat's emotions will soon die down."

"Really? I mean, she's just at the *start* of being a teenager—how do I know that her meltdowns won't get worse from here?"

"I can tell you from both the research and my own clinical experience that emotional intensity actually peaks around age thirteen or fourteen and then slowly tapers down from there."

"That," said Valerie, "is a huge relief. We spent the holidays thinking that we were seriously in for it if Nat's teenage moods were just getting started. It's good to hear that her emotionality may already be at max levels." Valerie reflected for a moment before adding, "But if her brain won't be fully developed until she's twenty-four, does that mean that she'll be acting like a teenager for eleven more years? That can't be right."

"True—that's not actually how it goes. People often become impressively mature long before young adulthood. The sophisticated regions of their brain *are* developing, they just lag a bit behind the ancient emotion centers."

I shared with Valerie that it always rubs me the wrong way when people dismiss teenagers wholesale by saying that their brains aren't fully developed. While this is true at the most technical level, it is impossible to look at some of the art, computer programs, music, or AP English papers produced by high school juniors and suggest that they are not the products of people with a highly developed brain.

"In fact," I went on, "by age fifteen, Nat will be able to reason as well as you or I can, provided that she's not wound up. The only issue is that the prefrontal part of her brain probably won't hit full strength until she's a young adult. Before then, her ability to maintain a sense of perspective may sometimes be knocked offline if she's having a highly charged emotional reaction."

"Good to know," Valerie said with relief, "and Nat will be glad to hear this herself. She was pretty freaked out by her meltdowns and I'm sure that she'll feel a lot better once she has a way to make sense of what's happening. She'll also be glad to hear that her emotions won't feel so out of control for long."

"Yes," I told her, "things should calm down. But now that she's a teenager, you, and she, are entering a whole new emotional landscape."

## Why Your Teen Hates How You Chew

A few years ago I picked up a message on my office voicemail from a mom named Rachel, who sounded as if she was at the end of her rope.

"I've been trying to get my daughter Anna to agree to therapy," the message explained, "but she flat-out refuses. So I'm wondering if my husband and I can make an appointment with you, because ever since Anna started eighth grade, she's been making life at home totally miserable. We're not sure what to do, but we need to do something."

I'm always happy to meet with parents and often find that it's a lot more productive to meet with adults who want help than to meet with a teenager who has decided that she doesn't. I called Rachel back, and we set up a lunchtime appointment that worked for her and her husband.

Once we settled into my office, Rachel, a midforties woman whose dark hair had a beautiful gray streak in the front, began.

"I got your name from the counselor at Anna's school, and I think the first thing you should know is that the counselor was puzzled by the fact that I was looking for help. When I explained that Anna was being incredibly unpleasant at home, he joked that he wasn't sure that we were talking about the same girl. He said that she's terrific at school—kind, attentive, funny—and that her teachers often say they wish they had ten more kids in class just like her."

"That's helpful to know," I said. "So what's the story at home?"

Rachel's husband, Mark, chimed in. "She really is a good kid. But she's often pretty icy and rude to us." As he spoke, Rachel shook her head slowly in a gesture that seemed to be a mix of frustration and despair. Mark adjusted his eyeglasses before gently adding, "Rachel actually gets the brunt of it. Anna doesn't give it to me like she gives it to her mom." Rachel nodded in wholehearted agreement.

"Can you give me an example of what's happening?" I asked.

"Sure," said Rachel. After reflecting for a moment, she began, "Okay, here's one. This may sound small, but it felt like shit. I was working in the living room on my computer when Anna was waiting for a friend to come over. First, Anna asked if I was going to stay in the living room or if I might take my work upstairs. I told her that I wasn't planning on moving. So then she said that she wanted me to change clothes before her friend came over, because the outfit I was wearing was 'dumpy.' I couldn't believe it—she was acting like such a snot."

"What did you do?" I asked. Rachel explained that she refused to change clothes or to move, and that Anna retaliated by giving her the cold shoulder for the rest of the day.

"Here's another one," she said. "Anna started watching *The Great British Baking Show* a few weeks ago and now has gotten really into baking. This is something I'm pretty good at and that we used to do together when she was little. The other day I saw her checking the expiration date on our baking soda, so I started to explain the chemistry behind how it goes bad. She quickly got surly and practically yelled, 'Oh my God, Mom, STOP!' and then stormed out of the kitchen as if I'd done something awful."

"I see," I said sympathetically. "What have you tried so far?"

Mark weighed in. "We've both told her that her behavior is totally out of line. But that hasn't made a difference. And we've gotten mad at her, but then she just holes up in her room. Eventually she'll come out, and when she does, she acts like nothing happened. There are also plenty of times when she's the kid we remember—the one who likes us and enjoys spending time with us. But it's as if we're living with Dr. Jekyll and Mr. Hyde. We never know who's coming out of her bedroom."

"I got so fed up with her the other day," added Rachel, "that I told her she needed to go to therapy to figure out what her problem was. That, obviously, didn't work. So here we are."

As I listened to Rachel and Mark's description of life at home with Anna, it was clear that their daughter was well under way with the developmental phase that we psychologists refer to as *separation-individuation*. While this dry term is technically fitting, I have always felt it vastly undersells the impact of having a young teenager in the throes of this particular process. If I were tasked with renaming this developmental phase so as to capture how it really plays out in family life, I'd probably go with something like "When parents become totally mortifying," or "The several months when your teenager can't stand how you chew."

Whatever we call it, this normal chapter of adolescent development can be really unpleasant for the adults involved, especially because it often comes on the heels of the friendly relationship that parents typically enjoyed with their latency-age child. The bad news is that this rocky phase is an all but guaranteed aspect of adolescence. The better news is that understanding what's behind behavior like Anna's makes it easier to know how to respond.

To begin with the separation side of the separation-individuation equation, building an identity that is distinct from that of your parents is a necessary part of healthy adolescent development. Anna, like most young teenagers, suddenly and appropriately wishes to distinguish herself from her mom and dad. She wants to establish, as it were, her own "brand." Anna may have ideas about the kind of brand she's looking to build, but she is young enough that her identity is still closely entwined with her parents'. This makes it annoying to her when her parents' branding doesn't line up with the emerging brand she envisions for herself. For Anna at thirteen, it can feel like a crisis to have her mom wearing a "dumpy" outfit in the presence of her friends. This is also why young adolescents suddenly become appalled by parental traits—our corny humor, our jazzy dance moves—that they enjoyed (or at least didn't mind) not so long ago.

On top of that, there's the individuation side. As young teenagers start to figure out their personal brands, it matters tremendously to them that their brands be wholly distinct from ours. The son of a friend of mine refused to play catch with his dad for most of the boy's fourteenth year. The dad is a talented athlete, and at fourteen, his son was actively organizing his identity around being a member of the high school's baseball team. For a stretch, the boy could not feel that baseball was "his thing" if he continued to practice with his dad. And this is why it rubbed Anna the wrong way when Rachel, herself a skilled baker, tried to support Anna's emerging identity as someone who liked to bake.

Together, separation and individuation amount to a guaranteed no-win situation for parents. As our teens are trying to become more separate, they are put off by our traits that *don't match* their emerging brand. And simultaneously, their efforts to establish their own brand cause teens to be annoyed when one of our traits *does match* their new identity. The sum of this equation? *Everything* we do is annoying.

After explaining all of this to Rachel and Mark, I said, "So even though Anna's behavior is pretty unpleasant—and we'll figure out what to do about it—how she's acting is also typical for her age. In other words, it's actually a lot less personal than it feels."

"But then why is she so much nastier with me than with her dad?" asked Rachel.

"I think for girls it can be harder to feel separate from their moms. They often feel closer to their mothers or more like them, and so they have to push away with more force."

"That makes sense . . . I think that part of what has made this so challenging is that we used to get along so well," said Rachel sadly.

"So what are we supposed to do?" asked Mark. "I'm not okay with her acting like this."

"Understandably," I said, "and it's not good for Anna to feel that she can get away with treating anyone badly, including you. My advice would be that when she's being unpleasant, try to engage as little as possible." I then paused for a moment before asking, "What would happen if, instead of responding to her rude behavior, you offered her three options for how she *can* interact with you? You could tell her she can be friendly, or that she can tell you what's wrong while being civil, or that she can let you know that she needs some space. Anything else, you could add, is off the table."

"We can give that a try," said Rachel. "But what if I've already blown it? The other day Anna stormed off to her bedroom over something tiny—I can't even remember what it was. I got so pissed that I shouted *'This feels like shit!'* through the closed bedroom door and then felt awful about having yelled at her."

"I get it," I said, "and you're hardly the first parent to lose your cool with a teen. My general rule is that when parents act in ways they regret, their best bet is to own it and apologize. I know this sounds corny, but you can take it as an opportunity to model for Anna how to make things right when she feels bad about her behavior."

"It would be great if she told us that she felt sorry," said Mark. "In the meantime, what are we supposed to do when she pretends like nothing happened and is nice to us not long after she's acted like a jerk? Should we just drop it?"

"That's a tough call. On the one hand, you might want to re-visit how she acted and perhaps ask her to apologize. On the other, there's a lot to be said for just enjoying her—and having her enjoy you—when she's being pleasant. You can try it both ways. The key here is to try not to hold a grudge. Teens' moods shift so quickly that it's easy to feel mad at them about some-thing that they've already forgotten. The more we can be with our teens where they are moment by moment, the better."

As we neared the end of our session, I reassured Rachel and Mark that time was on their side. Teenagers work hard at cultivating their emerging personal brand and often do so by throwing themselves into the things they care about. Adolescents get seri-ous about specific subjects at school, their sports, their artistic talents, other clubs and activities, or finding ways to make money.

As teens develop their own interests and skills, their indepen-dent identities are outlined and filled in, and they develop a healthy sense of standing apart from their parents. As this hap-pens, they tend to find us less embarrassing and become more inclined to view our quirks as a problem with *our* brand, not theirs. And once teens have had time to establish a real sense of ownership over their emerging identity—once they consolidate a sense of themselves as an amateur baker, a rising baseball player, or anything else—they can return to sharing those interests with us without feeling that it encroaches on the brand identity they have worked so hard to develop.

All in all, ages thirteen and fourteen can be especially chal-lenging for both teens and their parents. It's hard on everyone when teenagers' gawky brains cause peak emotionality right around the time that they really get going with the separation-individuation process. And although adolescents usually gain more emotional control as they age and outgrow their feeling of being personally affronted by their parents' idiosyncrasies, that doesn't mean that peace descends at home.

## Heightened Friction, and How to Deal with It

When our children are young, they almost invariably look up to us. But as they age into adolescence, aided by their new neurological power, they start to catch on to our shortcomings. On top of that, teens' normal drive to become separate from us compels them to see us from a new and removed perspective. Whereas they used to accept us without question, now they give us feedback. This has certainly played out in my own home. It has long been true that I lay down household policies that I believe in but don't always follow myself, such as not bringing a cellphone to the dinner table. Nor am I above resorting to guilt to get my way. But not until my daughters were teenagers did they begin to comment that I am "a total hypocrite" or, when I drop a passive-aggressive comment, to playfully retort "Get out the luggage—we're going on a guilt trip!"

As teenagers, they really have my number. At times I wonder, do they *really* need to itemize my imperfections? Sometimes loudly, and occasionally in anger? As a mom, I can definitely find such criticism hard to take. But as a psychologist, I get it. Here's why: Teenagers become keenly aware of our warts right around when they start readying themselves to leave home. Consciously or not, they realize that there's not much time left for us to become better parents while they are still under our roof.

This is a big issue for them. While they may enjoy excellent support from adults outside the family, they are very much aware that we're the only parents they'll ever have. Ideally, and in time, our kids will do what most people do: come to terms with the fact that there is no perfect parent and find a way to accept our shortcomings. But while they're still living at home, why wouldn't our teens try to improve the parenting hand they've been dealt?

Years ago, I was caring for the teenage son of a successful and domineering businessman. The boy and his father were constantly at odds, because the father approached parenting with the same controlling managerial style that he relied on at work. The son, understandably, did not welcome his father's attempts to micromanage his studies, and would angrily tell his dad to back off and trust that he was on top of his work. Which he was. The dad, for his part, thought his son was foolish to reject his sound guidance. I agreed with the boy, but that wasn't the point.

"I think you fight with your dad," I observed, "because you're hoping that if you point out what he's doing wrong, he'll change."

"Yeah, that's probably true," he said.

"So far, though, you've had no luck with that. Here are the options I see: You can keep fighting with him in hopes that he'll change, or we can invite him to join us for a session and I'll take a crack at it, or we can try to figure a way for you to live with his bossy style until you graduate."

The boy went with the third option. Our therapy turned toward helping him take his father's micromanaging less personally—indeed, the dad treated the boy's siblings similarly—and see that the father's behavior came from a loving place, even if it rubbed the boy the wrong way. Over time, my client gave up on the hope that his dad would treat him with more respect and acknowledge that he was indeed an organized and competent student. Letting go of that wish made it easier for him to enjoy the better aspects of his relationship with his father, such as their shared interest in fishing. The boy continued to clash with his dad from time to time, but only when getting into what he knew would be a fruitless fight felt easier to stomach than giving in.

Here's a personal pro tip: When your teenager points out your shortcomings, try to keep an open mind. In my experience, adolescents' descriptions of adults tend to be pretty spot-on. If we can tolerate their feedback, our teens may even help us grow. Should you be wondering whether your adolescent's critiques hold water, try asking a kind and clear-eyed partner or friend for a second opinion. Your teen might be telling you something that is worth trying to work on, even if they don't bring it to your attention in the nicest way.

I'm still trying to do better in the hypocrisy and passive aggression departments, but I can say that being a parent, especially of teenagers, is the best thing that has ever happened to my personality. For example—and thanks to my daughters' feedback—I have become vastly more relaxed about my petty concerns about the tidiness of our home. And, like me, you may have noticed that our teenagers also tend to be many steps ahead of us on topics related to social fairness and inclusion and quick to point out our blind spots or narrow-minded thinking. Our teenagers want us to be the best possible versions of ourselves, and we should want that, too.

There's another reason that being an adolescent contributes to more friction at home. In their age-appropriate wish to become more independent, they challenge our authority. Teens will want to do things we are reluctant to allow, such as hang out at a friend's house where we know from experience that the fun often gets out of control. Or they will refuse to do things we want them to do, like keep their clothes off their bedroom floor. It's unpleasant to butt heads with your teenager, but I am always more concerned when there's no teen-parent friction than when there is. If everybody is doing their job, teenagers will be pushing for more freedom and flexibility than their parents are inclined to allow, and parents will be pulling back on them, saying no to some requests and enforcing reasonable rules. If you find yourself living with this tension, take heart. It usually means that everything is going exactly as it should.

At times, parents and teens get stuck at loggerheads. A teenager might be sure that she can manage herself over at a friend's house where gatherings tend to get wild, while her parents might be equally sure that going over there is a terrible idea. Or a teen might feel that it's not his parent's business if he chooses to keep *his* clothes on the floor of *his* room, yet the parent—who may have paid for the clothes and be paying the rent as well—might disagree. As much as we'd rather not get into a standoff with our teenagers, disputes like these are inevitable, and we should treat them as valuable opportunities to teach our teenagers how to handle conflict. In fact, research shows that learning to have healthy disagreements at home contributes to a teenager's overall well-being and improves how they manage their relationships with others.

Let's make our aim not to avoid conflicts, but whenever possible, to have constructive ones. And the hallmark of a constructive conflict is that each party tries to view the situation from the other's perspective. An impasse can usually be avoided if a teen tries to imagine why her mom might not want her to spend time at a rowdy house, and if her mom tries to imagine why her daughter thinks it won't be a problem.

Importantly, the capacity to infer what another person might be thinking improves dramatically in adolescence. The ability to stand mentally in someone else's shoes blossoms as a result of the major renovation project under way in the adolescent brain. Due to their earlier onset of puberty, girls tend to be ahead of boys in the development of this capacity. For our daughters, perspective taking increases significantly around age thirteen, while for our sons it tends to improve around age fifteen.

If you find yourself at odds with your teenager, see whether your teen's growing cognitive abilities can be recruited to ease a standoff. Consider saying, "Let's do this. I'm going to try to describe the situation from your perspective. When I'm done, you're going to tell me what I'm missing and where I'm off track." Do your level best to articulate how you think your teenager sees the situation and then be open to feedback about what you left out or got wrong. As you can imagine, it makes a powerful impact on a teenager to hear a parent say, "I'm wondering if you're feeling that you've earned our trust and we should count on you to make good choices, even when you're at a house where things get out of hand," or "We know how busy you are—are you feeling like it's not a big deal if your room is messy, given that you're staying on top of everything else?"

Then ask your teenager to do the same for you. If you are earnest and open when it's your turn, it's likely that your teenager will return the favor. An adolescent might say, "I know that you just want me to be safe, so it's scary for you when I'm at a house where kids get crazy," or "When my clothes are all over the floor, it probably seems like I don't appreciate the fact that you buy me nice things." There's something about articulating a competing viewpoint—*in one's own words*—that almost invariably produces compassion for it. Taking time to think through and state our teenagers' positions helps to build empathy for where they are coming from. When your teenager does the same, it will help build their empathy for your take on the situation as well. Appreciating where the other person is coming from also helps by shifting the focus off the people disagreeing and onto the problem that needs solving. The exercise of describing each other's position will not magically resolve every dispute, but it will almost always make a resolution easier to achieve.

## Risk Seeking, and How to Keep Teens Safe

If you find it stressful to have a teenager, what you are experiencing lines up with a study showing that raising adolescents is even more emotionally demanding than caring for children under the age of five. If we think about what we've looked at in this chapter so far, it's easy to see why. Living with young people whose gawky brains make them prone to meltdowns, whose drive toward establishing their own brand makes them annoyed by how we breathe, and whose wish to improve us or to become more independent has them critiquing our shortcomings and bristling at our rules can be emotionally exhausting. But that's only the half of it. On top of all that, parents often worry that their teenagers will take dangerous risks.

This is not an irrational concern. Thanks to the grand renovation project under way in their brain, teens—more than children or adults—are drawn to novel and exciting experiences. Adolescence involves a rise in the availability of dopamine, a natural chemical associated with positive feelings, that makes novel and highly charged experiences especially enjoyable and alluring for teens. While the yearning for excitement rises quickly in adolescents, their capacity for suppressing impulses develops more slowly. The spike we see in teenage risk taking can be partially accounted for by the fact that, neurologically speaking, teenagers can be all gas and no brakes.

No wonder parenting teens is so stressful.

Despite the neurological realities of the teenage brain, there's still a lot parents can do to help keep them out of harm's way. Thinking back to the topic of cold and hot cognition from chapter 1, take advantage of the rational thinking that prevails in adolescents under "cold" conditions to strategize with them about how they will handle the risks that might arise in the socially and emotionally "hot" ones. For example, when a teenager mentions over dinner that she has plans to go to a concert with friends, use that time to have her sketch out the tricky situations that could arise and her plans for how she would handle them.

It's also important to recognize that, with regard to risk taking, the forces that act on teenagers from the outside are more influential than what's happening inside their brain. Research comparing adolescents from around the world has found that risk taking, such as experimenting with alcohol, varies widely despite the fact that teens everywhere have the same risk-prone neurology. Much of the variance comes down to local norms and the kinds of risks that are available. For me, the takeaway is that while you might not have much control over the conventions of your community, ensuring that teens have appropriate levels of supervision and limiting their ability to do dangerous things will make a material difference for their safety.

Studies also show that teenagers benefit from having high standards set for their behavior. When parents assume their teens will misbehave, adolescents tend to live down to those expectations. In contrast, parents who talk openly with their teens about the risks they might face and who articulate and enforce reasonable guidelines for behavior have teenagers who are less likely to drive recklessly, binge drink, try illegal drugs, or engage in unprotected sex. Accordingly, adults should let our teenagers know that we have faith in them and that we are always available to talk about the dangers they might encounter. Further, parents should have clear rules or expectations for how their teenagers will handle themselves when they are driving, given access to alcohol or drugs, or considering having sex. These conversations often go best when they're less about what *we* want for our teens and more about the priorities teens usually have for *themselves,* such as thriving academically or in their extracurriculars, or simply keeping future doors open by maintaining a clean school and legal record.

At the same time, we should do contingency planning with our teens for the possibility that they might find themselves in a situation that has gotten out of control. Some adults may worry that saying both "I don't want you to drink at parties" and also "If you get yourself in a jam around drinking, I'm here to help" sends a mixed message, but I don't think that's an issue. Teens, by their nature, can sometimes find themselves in unexpectedly dangerous situations. Our teenagers are aware of this, and we're more likely to keep the lines of communication open if we make it clear that we are aware of it too. "My hope is that you won't drink," you might say, "but I am realistic about the fact that mistakes get made. Nothing matters more than your safety. The easiest way to stay safe is to stay sober. But if that doesn't happen, I'm your safety plan."

I cannot argue enough for centering any discussion of risky behavior on the topic of safety. Of course we have good reasons to talk with teens about what we think is morally right and the trouble they could get into with the law. But our teens may not share our moral stance or may consider the laws regulating drugs or drinking to be nonsensical and may feel it unlikely that they'll get caught anyway. And while supervising adolescents can keep them safe, it would be impossible (and developmentally inappropriate) to try to monitor teens all the time. Focusing squarely on safety keeps the emphasis where it belongs. We love our teenagers, and we worry about their risky behavior not because it's "wrong," but because it's dangerous. To drive this point home, consider saying something along these lines: "If you're in a dicey situation, the last thing I want you to worry about is whether you could get *caught*. The main thing I want you to worry about is whether you could get *hurt*." From there, be clear that you will never, under any conditions, make your teen regret asking for your help.

Finally, adults should honor the fact that teenagers are neurologically primed to seek excitement and allow them some (perhaps carefully chosen) opportunities to satisfy their boundary-pushing needs. My teenage skitching was a bad idea, but the many days I spent skiing with my high school friends were developmentally ideal. When I turned sixteen, I bought myself a $900 car with money I earned busing tables. Early on Saturday mornings, that white diesel Volkswagen Rabbit and I would make the rounds to pick up my friends. We'd buy our discounted lift tickets at the local grocery store and then start the hour-and-a-half trip to our favorite mountain. Driving in what were often challenging conditions, we would happily sing along with the inappropriate lyrics coming from our favorite mixtapes. We'd spend the day finding slopes just beyond our skill level, resting only during lift rides, when we'd eat the sandwiches we'd packed in our coats. By the end of the day, we were physically spent, but our need to take chances, push boundaries, and seek thrills was thoroughly met.

Teens are built to search out new and exciting experiences. So let them. Some kids travel to unfamiliar parts of town to go thrifting with their friends, others work on increasingly daring skateboard tricks or get into camping, hiking, climbing, water sports, or the like. I cannot assure you that allowing teens to engage in activities that might fray adult nerves will keep them from making frightening mistakes. But I can definitely tell you that most teens need to satisfy their appetite for excitement and will do it one way or another. We cannot change our teen's desire to take some risks, but we can work to keep the lines of communication open about which boundary-pushing behaviors we can, and can't, live with.

## Starting Life Online

Adolescents are innately drawn to all that digital technology has to offer, because it gives them a new way to connect with their peers, feel independent, and—if they're so inclined—take a walk on the wild side. Given the many alarming headlines—and even congressional hearings—suggesting that digital activity can harm teenagers, parents may understandably worry about what time online means for their teen's emotional health. What do we know? In truth, the picture isn't clear. Some studies suggest a link between the rise of cellphone use and adolescent mental health problems, while other research fails to support this sweeping conclusion. And some studies indicate that digital technology can actually contribute to teens' overall sense of well-being.

This murkiness results from the fact that much of the research on teens and digital technology is *correlational*, meaning that it can establish a relationship between technology use and adolescent moods, but it can't prove that one of these variables *causes* the other. A correlation between cellphone use and teen depression could mean that teens who spend a lot of time on their cellphones are more likely to become depressed, or that teens who become depressed start spending a lot of time on their cellphones, or that a third factor (a global pandemic, for example) is causing teens to both spend more time on their phones *and* become more depressed.

Nonetheless, we have reason to think that, for most teenagers, time spent online can be both good and bad. Teens use texting and social media platforms to make meaningful connections, cultivate friendships, and enjoy harmless entertainment. It is also true that many of the same adolescents find that digital technology invites time wasting, unkind behavior, social comparison, and exposure to disquieting content. In my experience, teenagers will freely admit that they feel mixed about the place of digital technology in their lives. As one adolescent girl recently told me, "I love my phone. And I hate it too."

So how do we help teenagers minimize the downsides of their online lives? We do know that texting, sharing content, and commenting on other people's posts seem to boost adolescent well-being but that mindless scrolling likely contributes to emotional discomfort. In talking about this with a co-ed group of high school juniors I shared that, to me, going online feels like playing a slot machine. Sometimes I find something interesting or enjoyable. Sometimes I come across a post or headline that makes me upset. And often I scroll and scroll looking for something I can't quite name, and then end up feeling frustrated about the time I've wasted. The teenagers I was talking with said they felt the exact same way. Our shared experience allowed for a rich conversation about why it is that we decide to go online and whether it's always the best way to meet our needs to connect, find an enjoyable distraction, or get information.

That conversation went well, but often teens become immediately skeptical when adults try to weigh in on their online pursuits. Here, they have a point. Nobody parenting a teen today came of age attached to a device, and regardless of how addicted we now are to our own phones or computers, we do not use technology the way our teens do. Adolescents, like the rest of us, are usually reluctant to take advice from anyone who may not know what they're talking about. You might say that teens are likely to receive our guidance on managing their relationship with technology about the same way we would their guidance on refinancing our mortgage.

To account for this, ask a lot of questions, though not all at once ("Too many questions!!!" is the number one complaint I hear from my own teenagers). Over time, try to learn what your teenager enjoys most about being online, and what's annoying, frustrating, or unsettling. Ask what, if anything, your teen has done to try to make the time spent online more positive. And, if you're an avid tech user, talk openly about how you've navigated the same challenges yourself.

How else can you minimize the harms of the virtual world? Help your teen understand the algorithm-driven nature of online content. Teenagers don't always recognize that their online experience is heavily shaped by what they've searched for or "liked." As soon as any of us looks for information on a specific topic or engages with posts related to a particular subject, algorithms behind media platforms start to flood our feeds with similar content in order to keep an iron grip on our attention. This might be fine for an adolescent searching for crafting how-tos, sports news, videos of popular dances, or hilarious memes. But this can be a huge problem if a teen becomes curious about white supremacy, conspiracy theories, or dieting fads. It's not simply the case that teenagers sometimes fall down creepy or dangerous digital rabbit holes. Online media is designed to *pull* their users down rabbit holes.

Talk openly with your teenager about the fact that digital platforms are manipulative by design. Teenagers are aware of this insofar as they aptly describe social media apps as having many "sides"—using this term to capture the truth that algorithms push different content to different users. Teens, by their nature, prize their autonomy and don't like to be jerked around by adults. Use this to your and your teen's advantage. Point out that "Online platforms have one goal—to keep you engaged for as long as possible. They collect data on what you're interested in and decide what you see—whether it's healthy for you or not."

How close an eye should you keep on what your teen is consuming online? You know your adolescent best. If you trust that algorithms won't get the better of your teenager, go with your gut until you have a reason not to. If you're worried that your teen might get sucked down a problematic rabbit hole, come up with a supervision plan. Options could include having access to your teen's media accounts or enlisting a trustworthy older sibling or cousin to do the job. If your teenager balks, ask for—and be open to—your teen's suggestions for helping them stay on the right side of online content.

## Keeping Technology in Its Place

A healthy relationship with technology doesn't hinge just on how teens are using it and what they're looking at. It also comes down to how much space technology takes up in their lives. Here are some basic rules that can make a substantial difference: When first giving adolescents access to digital devices, go slow. Most tweens need little more than the ability to text, so that they can connect with their friends. If you decide to allow them to use social media, consider doing so only with the right to monitor their activity closely, at least in the beginning, and to limit how much time is spent socializing online. Don't hesitate to start with rigid rules. Tweens and teens are usually so eager to embark on their virtual lives that they will agree to stringent parameters just to get started. You can also set boundaries for when and where devices can be used, and observe the same parameters yourself. Keeping meals, short car rides, and family activities tech-free can be a great way to start.

I also strongly believe that digital technology should not be in anyone's bedroom, especially overnight. While some teenagers need to do their homework in their room, once it's time to go to sleep, they can be expected to charge their laptops, phones, and any other digital tech elsewhere. I appreciate that this might seem like a Draconian approach to regulating devices, but hear me out. First, we have clear evidence from large-scale surveys that having technology in the bedroom overnight undermines sleep, a resource that is already in short supply for most adolescents. Second, using devices behind closed doors at any time of day or night seems to me to invite trouble. Teenagers can certainly wade into dangerous digital waters while sitting in our kitchen or den, but overall it's less likely when we can walk by at any moment. Further, it's all too easy for teens to make dumb or destructive mistakes when they're up late and their neurological brakes are tired. Why allow conditions where your kid can make an impulsive, but lasting, error at one in the morning?

There's also the not small issue of pornography. Several years ago, I was invited to give a speech to the parents of a Catholic parish school in my community. I knew that my presentation would include guidance on talking about sex, and so, before giving my talk, I reached out to the pastor of the parish. As his guest, I wanted to be sure that he was comfortable with my deliberately frank approach to the normal, but understandably touchy, issue. After I previewed for him the guidance I encourage adults to offer young people on sex and romance, he replied, "Oh, yes, please say all of that. Also, I need you to talk about porn." Noticing my surprise, he explained, "I take confession from a lot of high school boys, and you would not believe how many of them tell me that they watch porn online late into the night. They feel horrible about it but cannot get themselves to stop."

This I understood. Online pornography is so accessible that 93 percent of boys and 62 percent of girls are exposed to it by age seventeen. And if you are not familiar with the pornography that is digitally available, you should know that much of it is raw, graphic, and often centered on themes of violence and degradation. Porn is titillating, even when it's dark and upsetting, so it was easy for me to imagine that the boys in the confessional could feel awful about what they were looking at, yet unable to resist it. Of course, keeping tech out of teens' bedrooms won't solve the issue of pornography altogether. But limiting access to technology overnight can help keep teens from feeling out of control around content that can leave them feeling very uneasy. Limiting access to pornography can also protect their enjoyment of real-life physical intimacy, which, research shows, can be undermined by watching porn.

## Peer Relationships, Both Romantic and Not

The arrival of adolescence brings with it the possibility of a love life, and many young people feel nervous as they imagine how they will find their way in what can feel like a strange new territory. Here, parents can help calm adolescent nerves and, above all else, introduce the idea of what healthy romantic relationships look like. Listen for when your teen puts the topic of romance on the table, perhaps by asking you a direct question about dating, but more likely by wanting to watch a sappy rom-com or mentioning that a friend now has "an official girlfriend." Capitalize on those moments to make the point that the healthiest romances are the ones that layer amorous intimacy over genuine friendship. This approach returns teens to familiar territory and helps them set off on their love lives in the best possible way.

To deepen these conversations, you can talk in specific terms about what makes for any good relationship, whether it's a friendship or a romance. Healthy relationships are equitable, kind, and enjoyable; unhealthy relationships are lopsided, harsh, or stressful. More than anything, healthy relationships *feel* good. They are warm and energizing and bring out the best aspects of our personality. In contrast, unhealthy relationships leave us feeling anxious or uneasy, or bring to the surface the traits in ourselves that we like least. The parallels between healthy romances and healthy friendships can seem obvious once articulated, but teenagers often need adults to point them out.

In the spring of his junior year of college, I heard again from Tom, my oboe-playing client who chose for himself a college close to home. He texted me to see if we could set up a virtual appointment. I hadn't heard from Tom for a couple of years. The last report was when, during his sophomore year, I ran into his mom at the grocery store and she told me how well he was doing. We found a time and got on a call. Tom let me know that he continued to be very happy at school, but that he was troubled by how his relationship with a young woman at his college was going.

"I don't know how to read this, or what to do," he explained. "Most of the time she's really fun and supportive, but pretty often she'll ghost me for days." He shared that they had met through friends and been hanging out, and making out, for a few months. "Things will seem fine, but then she'll disappear and I don't know what I did wrong."

"Have you asked her about it?"

"Yeah," he said. "When I text and don't hear back from her, I'll ask if everything's okay. Then she'll tell me that she's mad at me, but she won't say why."

"So what do you do?" I asked.

"I'll leave her alone for a little while, and then she'll reach out and want to study together. She'll act all normal and won't want to talk about what happened."

"Have you let her know that this is a problem for you?"

"Yeah," he said. "I spent a long time writing her a text saying that I liked her, but that I wanted to be able to talk about it when things weren't good between us. She pretended like she never got it and just went back to being fun."

"Do you want to stay in this relationship? Does it feel good to you?"

"Kinda. When things are good, I really like her. But when I can't figure out what's happening, it feels super uncomfortable."

"Let's think about it this way." I said, "What would you do if a friend acted like that?"

"It would bother me. I probably wouldn't make a big thing of it, but I also wouldn't try to keep the friendship. I'd just hang out with other people instead."

"I think you should apply that same standard here. Relationships are relationships—and you shouldn't put up with anything from someone you're dating that you wouldn't put up with from a friend."

"I get it," said Tom, "but I also get it that it's sometimes complicated when you're part of a couple."

"This is true—conflict comes with any close relationship. But there's good and bad conflict. The good kind happens when people are able to talk openly and respectfully about the problem. When there's blaming, attacking, avoidance, or discussing the issue with other people instead of addressing it within the relationship, that's the bad kind.

"It's easy to get along when things are good," I added. "The real measure of a friendship or romance is what happens when things get rocky. It seems like you've done a good job of pushing for a healthy way to address the problem, but it doesn't sound like she's able to meet you there."

"Yep, that's how it feels. So what do you think I should do?"

"That's your call," I said, "but when it comes to the relationships that we get to choose—who we're friends with and who we date—I'm all for holding both to high standards. My sense is that you wouldn't treat anyone this way, so I don't think you want to be in a relationship where you're treated like this."

Tom and I connected again the following week, and in that

conversation, he let me know that he'd made another effort to talk with his girlfriend about her running so hot and cold with him.

"I got nowhere," he said. "We were on the phone and she just kept saying that she didn't want to talk about it, and then tried to change the subject."

"So what did you do?"

"Nothing at the time. But I was really frustrated, so I sent her a text saying that if we couldn't talk about our problems, we probably shouldn't be going out. I haven't heard from her since."

"Have you broken up?" I asked.

"I think so. And I don't feel good about how it happened. I wish it hadn't been by text."

"When will you see her again?"

Tom paused a moment before responding, "Some friends of ours are having a party soon, so I might see her there."

"If you don't hear back from her sooner, maybe you could say something when you see her—maybe about wishing that things had ended in a better way and apologizing that you texted something that would probably have been better saved for a conversation."

"I could. But that will be really awkward."

"Yes, it probably will," I said, "but you might feel better if you apologize for the part you don't feel good about."

Tom agreed, and we set up an appointment for a couple of weeks later in which I learned that he'd seen his former girlfriend at the party and that they'd talked briefly.

"I let her know that I felt bad that we didn't really sort things out. And she said she felt bad too. I think we're okay with each other, and I'm glad it's over and that I'm not worrying about it all the time like I was before. It does help to remind myself that I wouldn't keep a friendship that made me feel so uneasy, so I shouldn't try to hold on to a girlfriend who does."

• • •

Suggesting to teens that healthy romances are healthy friendships plus physical intimacy might strike them as quaint or even antiquated. But hold your ground. Whenever teenagers tell me that meaningless one-night stands or friends-with-benefits arrangements are now the fashion, I push back with a few key points.

First, I let them know that despite the media hype, hook-up culture is not actually the norm. Survey data show that most adolescents are *not* having casual sex, and that most adolescents would prefer to have sex in the context of a meaningful relationship, not a passing fling. Second, I let them know that I get that combining emotional and physical intimacy in a single relationship can be extremely intense. I acknowledge that people can be wary of putting themselves in such a vulnerable position and that trying to separate emotional closeness from physical closeness can seem like a solution. But in fact, it typically isn't. Friends-with-benefits arrangements don't usually work out the way people hope, as very few of us can make out or have sex with someone without getting our feelings involved. Finally, it's much, much easier to communicate about who wants to do what physically—and to avoid a nonconsensual interaction—when sexual intimacy happens in the context of a caring and connected relationship. Yes, teens may at times insist that such views are old-fashioned, but I also know that they find great comfort in the idea that romance isn't dead, and that what they already know about how to have a good friendship can be carried over into having a good romance.

In practice, teens are all over the map with regard to what's happening in their love life. Some end up in powerful relationships that are as intimate as any marriage. Others date a little but don't find themselves involved in anything serious. Some finish high school without even so much as flirting with an agemate. So how do you talk about having a healthy love life with a teenager who, for one reason or another, just isn't there yet? Again, focus on the quality of your teenager's friendships.

As one insightful study found, it's what's happening in teens' nonromantic relationships, not their adolescent dating experiences, that lays the groundwork for a happy adult romantic life. Researchers followed a group of young people from ages thirteen to thirty to determine which factors predicted a gratifying love life as an adult. They found that adult romantic happiness was linked not to adolescent romantic activity, but instead to the friendship skills teenagers were developing along the way. Who went on to have a healthy adult love life? Generally speaking, those who, at age thirteen, expected to be treated well by friends and were able to respectfully stand up for themselves when necessary. And those who, at ages fifteen and sixteen, were able to establish close friendships and get along with peers. And those who, at seventeen and eighteen, were able to maintain close friendships over a two-year period. Keeping an eye on these benchmarks will help you know that your teen is coming along in developing the skills needed for healthy romances down the line.

There's no typical version of a teenage love life, and matters can be even more complicated for teens who are not straight or who are gender-expansive. They may need to hide how they feel if they are coming of age in families or communities that are unlikely to support their romantic choices. Or they may need more time to gain clarity on what they want for themselves, given that their love life doesn't fit with the dominant script. And while some teenagers have adult role models for gratifying and enriching LGBTQ+ romantic relationships, not all will, leaving them to figure out a healthy love life on their own.

Regardless of how teens identify, having strong peer connections is good for them in the near term and it helps them practice the kind of emotional intimacy that will lead toward having a fulfilling romantic life. If your teen seems to be struggling to make and keep friends, you'll want to understand what's getting in the way. If you need to, seek guidance from either a counselor at school or a mental health professional in your community.

## Why Teenagers Dislike School

Before adolescence, kids generally like school. But I think it's fair to say that if each household were to create a pie chart titled "Stuff Our Teen Complains About," the biggest slice in most homes would be labeled school. To be sure, there's plenty about school that teenagers *do* like, such as being with their friends, enjoying particular courses, and spending time with devoted teachers and coaches who truly care for them and don't try to hide it. But the fact of the matter is that school, by its nature, often cuts across the adolescent grain. Teens, now that they are getting serious about their autonomy, bristle at having to submit to adult authority all day long. And just when they are working to develop their freestanding and well-defined identity, they're herded into classes that often don't align with what they see as their brand. On top of all that, teenagers crave independence, but they often have loads of homework that prevent them from spending their evenings and weekends the way they want to.

How can adults help adolescents manage the mismatch between their normal drive for autonomy, identity, and independence and what school asks of them? I think we're most useful when we bear in mind that sending our teens to school is like sending them to a buffet where they are required to try everything being served. As adults, many of us have figured out what we like and what we don't, and we select for ourselves accordingly. In my case, I happily consume psychology all day and haven't had a bite of physics since I was seventeen. Teenagers, however, must consume everything on the menu. There is no way they will like all of it, and we should not expect that they will. I find that the school-as-mandatory-buffet metaphor brings needed neutrality to the loaded topic of academic motivation, so I'm going to risk beating it into the ground.

Let me start by saying that I think it's perfectly okay to require teenagers to dig into everything, in part because they may discover aspects of school that they end up, thanks to inspired teaching or their maturing interests, liking far more than they expected to. And so we should encourage them to be open to the possibility that they might enjoy a class they don't want to take or an experience they weren't looking forward to. Still, students will have their preferences, and when we acknowledge them and talk openly about them, we are better positioned to help teens maintain motivation at school.

Consider a common scenario: the teenager who strongly dislikes a class and as a result is significantly underperforming in it. Though our instincts might tempt us to tell such a teen to "fix his attitude," I think it's usually more helpful to start with a matter-of-fact conversation about the nature of school. "I get it," you might say. "You feel about English class right now the way I feel about beets. I eat them only when I have to, which, as an adult, is almost never." From there, you can point out that even if your teen can't stand this subject, selective high schools and colleges, scholarship committees, and future employers are usually at *least* as interested in students' grades as in their passions. "No one says you have to like English," you might add, "but we need to come up with a solution that makes the class palatable enough that you get a decent grade."

I don't want to diminish the inherent value of a school requirement or the satisfaction it might be able to bring, but sometimes teens need our help to get unstuck. For some, simply offering this kind of validation can be enough to fix the problem. For others who need more, framing their underperformance as an issue of taste, as opposed to a shortcoming in character, can lead to productive conversations about what might help them be more open to what's being served. Would they like, for instance, to try working with a study buddy or to look online for videos about what they're learning? If you suspect that there may be a significant barrier at work—perhaps the need to shore up missed content or an evaluation for a learning disorder—work with your teen's teachers or guidance counselors to find a solution that addresses the problem while keeping shame out of it.

If it won't rub your teenager the wrong way, you can also feel free to note that our tastes often change over time. I couldn't stand cilantro in high school, but I like it now; I took little interest in history back then, but I now read it every night before bed. "For now," you might say, "let's figure out how you can get what you need from this class. But going forward, I hope you'll keep an open mind about English. You might come to like it or find a teacher who dishes it up in a way that you really enjoy."

What about the adolescent who doesn't like *any* of what's on the middle or high school menu? This happens. School focuses on a very narrow range of topics and skills, and it is not at all unusual for a student to plod through a conventional education yet be poised to thrive in a career that is not rooted in traditional schooling. If this is your teenager, do these three things:

First, support your teen's interests where they lie. Does your teenager feel indifferent about her classes but have a hearty appetite for working with her hands? Find an in-school or after-school program that helps her build those skills. Does he take only sparing bites of the standard subjects but produce music on his own time? Then look for classes, jobs, or other opportunities to feed that interest.

Second, go out of your way to empathize with the fact that it's no fun to spend days, nights, and weekends consuming unappealing fare. Appreciate the effort that your teenager does put into school and recognize that doing so may not come easily or naturally.

Third, get help from a school counselor or other mental health professional to rule out depression or a substance use disorder. Healthy teenagers tend to cultivate strong interests, even if those interests aren't academic. If that isn't happening, you'll want to address the possibility of a broader mental health concern.

We should also pay attention to highly conscientious teenagers who feel compelled to devour every scrap of what's served. There's nothing wrong, of course, with students enthusiastically partaking in all that school has to offer. But learning can become unnecessarily stressful for teenagers who feel the need to excel on every assignment in every course. To combat needless perfectionism, once again, work from the buffet metaphor. "No one expects you to like every subject, or to like all of your classes equally. If you love math and want extra helpings, have at it. But if you're not into social studies, I think you should consume only as much as you need, whether for a high enough grade or deep enough mastery, while protecting your time and energy for other things—like sleep and having fun."

As parents, we need to be ready to adjust to the new emotional spin that adolescence puts on everyday life. If you reflect on what we've covered in this chapter, there's truly an extraordinary amount that changes as our children turn into teens. Adolescents walk around with a massive, destabilizing renovation project going on inside their skull. They suddenly feel compelled to separate from us and to build their own unique brand. At the same time, they must come to terms with our personal shortcomings and household rules and also figure out how to manage new sources of excitement and risk ranging from parties, drinking, drugs, and driving to social media, sex, and romance. On top of all that, school becomes freighted in new ways.

Even when the emotions involved in normal adolescent development are unpleasant, unwanted, or troublesome, they can still be the ones that make the best sense in the moment. What really matters is that adolescents learn to *manage* their disruptive feelings effectively. Let's now address how to help them do just that.

■ ■ ■ ■ ■

## CHAPTER FOUR

# Managing Emotions, Part One: Helping Teens Express Their Feelings

I opened my waiting room door on a Thursday afternoon in March to collect sixteen-year-old Jada for our appointment. Jada had recently gotten her license and now drove herself to our sessions. Carrying only her car keys, she slowly got up from the chair in my waiting room to follow me into my office. I could tell from the way she was moving that something was weighing her down.

We had first started meeting the previous November, when Jada's parents had become worried that she was depressed. Jada was having trouble sleeping, was often despondent, and struggled to focus on her schoolwork. She never did meet the full diagnostic criteria for clinical depression, but we made a strong connection and our work brought to light the worries she had about how she fit in at school and how she measured up against her impressive older sister. Once we were in the rhythm of weekly sessions, Jada's mood improved substantially. Given that several members of her extended family had been diagnosed with depression, Jada's parents were glad to support our ongoing regular meetings even though their daughter was now generally feeling pretty good.

On this particular Thursday, however, Jada sat heavily on my couch. I waited quietly for her to get us started as she pulled her long braids over one shoulder, fiddled with her necklace, then ran her hands over her tight, pre-ripped jeans.

"Today was awful," she began. "The casting came out for the spring musical—I tried out for the lead, but I got stuck in the chorus." She learned this when her drama teacher, who had done the casting, found her during a free period and asked to talk privately. "She told me that she really likes my singing, that she understood that the role I got wasn't the one I wanted, and that there would be two more musicals before I graduated and lots of time for me to grow as a performer."

I nodded reassuringly, then asked Jada how she had responded to her teacher.

"Actually, I cried when she told me. She was really nice about it and got me some water. But then I had to pull myself together because I had a quiz the next period." Jada explained that when she completed the quiz she asked to be excused to use the restroom. "I went into a stall and cried some more, but then I had to pull it together again to go to my last period class."

I took in Jada's description of her day with a mix of sympathy and admiration. On the one hand, I just hated to picture Jada sitting alone in a bathroom stall crying. On the other hand, her account of the afternoon—one in which she alternated between weeping and "pulling it together"—captured perfectly what it means to have the right feelings at the right time and to *manage them effectively*. Yes, intense, unwanted emotions are unpleasant, but they are part of life, and when they hit, we psychologists are really concerned with only one question: How well are those feelings being handled?

To return to the central premise of this book, mental health is not about feeling good. Distress comes with being human, and it certainly comes with being a teenager dealing with the challenges and disappointments that are part of growing up. When our teens become upset, our goal should be to help them manage their emotions well. The term psychologists use for the ideal management of feelings is *emotion regulation*. The body of research behind this concept is massive, but it can be organized under two basic headings: (1) gaining relief from destabilizing emotions by finding healthy ways to *express them*, and (2) when necessary, taking a break from unwanted emotions by using healthy tactics to *rein them in*.

It's beyond our power to prevent or quickly banish our teens' psychological pain, nor should that even be our goal. We can and should, however, help our teenagers develop ways to regulate their emotions that offer relief and do no harm. Jada did this beautifully, drawing on both emotional expression and emotional control to handle her disappointment over not getting the part she wanted. She cried in the presence of a caring teacher (healthy expression), then pushed the pause button on her sadness to take a quiz (healthy control). She excused herself to find a private place to cry a bit more (healthy expression), regained her composure to get through her last class (healthy control), and used her session with me to talk about her disappointment and frustration (healthy expression). What might look like a rough afternoon to anyone else looks like a master class in emotional regulation to those of us who help young people handle their feelings for a living.

Expression and control, control and expression. Most of the time, teenagers work out the needed balance on their own, as Jada did. But not always. Sometimes teens struggle to find appropriate outlets for their emotions, and sometimes their emotions run roughshod over everything else and need to be reined in. In either of these cases there's a definite need—and fortunately lots of room—for adults to step in and help.

I appreciate that this may be a new and unfamiliar way to think about how to help teenagers deal with uncomfortable feelings. But remember this: As parents we cannot prevent emotional pain in our teenagers. Rather, we should be in the business of helping them manage discomfort when it comes. Taking a management, not banishment, approach to unwanted feelings accomplishes exactly what parents of adolescents should be aiming for. We strengthen our connections to our teenagers when we come to notice and admire the very impressive work they are already doing to regulate their emotions. Further, we equip our teenagers for *independent* emotional lives by helping them learn to regulate their feelings effectively. And we set them up for *full* emotional lives as well, so they won't live in fear of strong feelings.

Think of this chapter and the next as giving you the emotional regulation playbook in two complementary volumes. Volume 1 (this chapter) will guide you in helping teenagers express their emotions in order to make them more bearable. Volume 2 (the next chapter) will be the playbook for helping teenagers take a break from their feelings as needed, to, in Jada's words, "pull themselves together" when it's time.

Why does the emotional expression playbook come first? Because finding an appropriate outlet for feelings almost always on its own provides our teenagers with all of the psychological relief they need. So let's get to it.

## Talking About Feelings Works

We take it as a given that putting feelings into words brings emotional relief. Conventional wisdom and personal experience tell us that "getting something off our chest," or "venting," or "talking about what's *really* going on" helps us feel better. But if you think about it, we should stand back in wonder at the fact that simply describing an uncomfortable psychological state somehow makes that state easier to bear. Though my entire career as a clinical psychologist rests on the assumption that finding words for emotions eases suffering, I've never quite gotten over the magic of this phenomenon.

Well, it's not exactly magic, and there are a number of theories about why putting feelings into words reduces psychological discomfort. One is that we can only gain insight, and thus relief, when we move emotions from the realm of abstract experience to the realm of language and thought. Another is that talking about painful feelings reduces our sense of isolation by allowing us to inform others of our otherwise invisible internal realities. We may still be awash in misery even after we've told someone about it, but it's usually better not to be entirely alone with our distress. In truth, psychologists have not come to broad agreement about why, exactly, we usually end up feeling better when we tell people that we're feeling lousy. But differing theories aside, we know that talking about feelings works. Beyond the abundant evidence of the effectiveness of talk therapy, we can measure the benefits of verbalizing emotions even at the physiological level.

In one study, research participants looked at upsetting photographs of natural disasters, gruesome accidents, or people in obvious agony. Then some of them were instructed to talk about their own emotional responses to the images, while others were told to simply state facts about the pictures. As the subjects either shared their personal feelings or presented objective facts, electrodes measured their emotional arousal via the electrical activity of their skin. Data from the electrodes showed that talking about the *feelings* brought on by the images had a calming effect, but describing the *facts* did not.

Another study used a similar approach to look at what happens in the brain itself when we give voice to how we're feeling. Researchers again asked volunteers to view distressing pictures and, in this study, instructed some to remain silent and others to describe how it felt to look at the images. As they looked at the pictures, the research participants' brains were monitored using *positron emission tomography,* a technology that allows for the observation of neurological activity in real time. Once again, the act of talking about feelings was shown to have a calming effect—this time on the activity of the amygdala and other parts of the brain associated with emotional arousal—while staying silent did not.

So, conventional wisdom about the benefit of talking about feelings is scientifically confirmed. Which brings us to a practical point in the parenting of teenagers: When we are actually faced with teens telling us just how very uneasy they are, we need to remember that their descriptions of their emotional pain—which may be vivid and dire-sounding—don't add to their emotional distress, but usually reduce it. It's critical to remember that by the time teens are *telling* us that they feel anxious or angry or sad or any other emotion they choose to put into words, they're already using an effective strategy for helping themselves cope with it. As a psychologist, I know this through and through. As a parent, though, I often forget it. When bedtime is approaching and one of my girls wants to talk about something that's been bothering her all day, I'm likely to think "Oh no! Where is this coming from?" rather than recognizing that she's already done the remarkable work of noticing her emotional discomfort, reflecting on it, giving that feeling a description, and then bringing it to me. What I often fail to appreciate on the spot is that she's already carried her emotional football all the way to the one-yard line. In the heat of the moment, I can make the mistake of focusing on *why* she's holding this football and on how I can get her to drop it as quickly as possible. But when I get it right, I recognize how much yardage she has gained on her own and that she's made it easy for me to help her over the goal line of relief.

## Listening, *Really* Listening, Matters

So, when teenagers tell us they are in psychological pain, what's our best response? Usually, it's simply to listen to what they have to say. This may seem obvious and easy on paper, but it can be surprisingly difficult to do in reality. We hate to see our teens suffer, and reflexively we attempt to ease their distress by trying to chase from the field whatever caused it. A teen says she doesn't like the timing of the shifts she's been assigned at work, and we tell her that she should talk to her manager. A teen is angry that a classmate swooped in and stole his prom date, and we list off other classmates he could ask. A teen complains about missing a best friend who is away at camp, and we offer reassurance that a letter is sure to come any day.

There's nothing wrong with any of these suggestions, but as you have likely learned from personal experience, they usually don't go over well. That's because we've focused our attention on the wrong target. Instead of trying to erase the problem that caused our teenager to become upset, we should see—at least at first—whether the act of putting feelings into words provides all the relief that is needed. Simply talking about feelings reduces their intensity, so let your teenager talk. Before you jump in with reassurance, a piece of advice, or a recollection of having had a similar experience a million years ago when you were a teenager, see what happens if you *just listen*.

Let me say right here that it's easy to think we're listening when we're really not. Instead of listening, we are often waiting for our teenager to finish talking so that we can share a thought that came to mind soon after our teen got started. That's not listening, that's turn taking. To *really* listen, imagine that you are a newspaper editor and that your teenager is one of your reporters, reading you a draft of a newspaper article about an aggravating teacher, or a classmate she's worried about, or some other troubling news of the day. Here's your task: As soon as your reporter comes to the end of the article, you have to craft its headline. In other words, you need to distill a long and detailed story down to its compelling essence. This takes real effort, but it is worth a try.

Though I often misstep in my own home, here's an example of a time I got it right: In March 2020, when the pandemic began, my older daughter was a sophomore in high school. As the realities of lockdown set in, she launched into a justified rant about what school had become. She railed about how they had taken away everything fun—the clubs, the games, the getting to be with friends—but left intact the lectures and the cramming for AP tests. I listened like an editor, and when she was finally spent, I said: "It sounds like school is now all vegetables and no dessert." She appreciated and accepted that headline and, at least for the time being, felt better. Putting her frustration into words and then hearing me use *my* words to encapsulate her experience was enough to bring her discomfort down to a tolerable level.

Don't worry if you can't come up with a headline, but do try. The act of paying this kind of attention to your reporter's story actually does its own good. It's rare for any one of us to put the full force of our concentration behind listening to what someone else is trying to communicate. Your teenager will notice, consciously or not, that you have truly tuned in and will find that comforting. When we engage fully and yet also refrain from pushing solutions, we wordlessly communicate three essential pieces of information: One, that we understand their emotional pain and are not alarmed by it, and so, two, they do not need to be afraid of it either. And three, that instead of playing Whac-a-Mole with their problems by firing off suggestions, we're providing something better: our attentive and steady presence.

## Empathy Goes Further than We Think

All right, you've listened and you've headlined and your teenager still isn't feeling much better? Here's your next play: Offer empathy. Merely extending our compassion is a proven way to help our teenagers, and yet it's an approach we often forget. Research shows that teens with empathetic parents actually have lower levels of systemic inflammation—a biological marker of emotional stress—but we tend to breeze right past offering empathy and instead serve up reassurance. It can seem almost too simple to just gently say "I'm so sorry to hear that," or "What you're describing sounds awful," or "No wonder you're feeling so down." But we should not assume that something so simple must be ineffective, especially given that we're trying to encourage our teenagers to regard talking about feelings as an indispensable way to regulate their emotions.

Whenever our own adolescents succeed in articulating their ups and downs, we want our response to reward and reinforce that behavior. Listening attentively and then offering empathy shows them that they are doing exactly the right thing when they seek relief by finding a loving listener (that would be us!) and sharing what's on their mind.

The next time your teenager feels miserable, respond with empathy. But do even more than that: Deliver your empathetic words with the full confidence that *your compassion alone* may deliver sufficient psychological relief. Recently I ran into a mother in my community who shared that she'd gotten serious about the utility of empathy after hearing me give a talk about treating compassion as a solution unto itself. "The other night my sixth grade daughter was devastated about being placed in a lower level math class than the one all of her friends are in," she said. "After she vented for a while, I said 'I get why you feel so terrible. What you're describing would leave *anyone* feeling rotten.' With that alone, her shoulders dropped and she relaxed. The next step," my friend half-joked, "is to get my husband to stop telling her that she'll be fine or that she can make friends in her new math class."

Even knowing that offering empathy goes very far, it can be hard to summon a tender response for everything adolescents bring our way. This can be especially true when we're at the end of our own long day and what our teenager wants to share is a litany of complaints. When I'm hustling to get dinner on the table and to keep the evening moving along so that I can wind down before bed, I often find that my fatigue is high and my empathy is low. At the literal end of the day, it can be a challenge for me to bring my parenting A game when one of my girls starts grousing about what happened at school. At these times, here's what gets me through: I take myself back to an auditorium in New Jersey where, many years ago, I was wrapping up a conversation about stress and anxiety with an audience of high school students.

"Before we finish," I said, "I have a question for you. Since I'm going to be giving a talk on this topic to your parents tonight, when I'm with them, is there anything you want me to pass along?" Several hands went up, including one belonging to a ninth grade girl with an earnest look on her face, who clearly had something pressing to say.

When I called on her, she stood and made her request: "Please tell them that when I complain about my school day, the *only* thing I want them to say back is, 'Oh my God, that stinks!'" Many of her classmates nodded in vigorous agreement, and some even applauded.

The parental reply that this ninth grader wanted to the exclusion of all others is now my default response to end-of-day complaining. I promise you, it will almost always provide the validation and support that teenagers need to feel better.

Yet even with this trusty response at my disposal and its long track record of working well, I still manage to blow it sometimes. Not long ago, my younger daughter came home from school unhappy about the fact that she would spend most of the next day taking standardized tests. When I started to rattle off reassurance that she could handle it and suggestions for how she might maintain her focus throughout the day, she looked at me quizzically and said, "Can't I just get a 'That stinks!'?"

## Helping Teens Get Specific About Feelings

The more precise teenagers can be when articulating their feelings, the bigger the benefit they'll get. Psychologists refer to making fine-grained distinctions among individual feelings as *emotional granularity*, and research demonstrates that being able to describe inner experiences with precision is associated with better emotional regulation and better mental health overall. Improving specificity puts the power of verbalizing feelings on steroids. Saying "I'm feeling despondent" brings more relief than saying "I'm sad." And remarking that "I feel bitter about what happened" dispels more distress than "I'm mad."

While teenagers often brim with emotions, they don't always know how to name what's happening inside and sometimes need help arriving at the most apt description. Though I've understood this point for as long as I've been a psychologist, I gained a new perspective on it while reading Jane Austen's *Pride and Prejudice* a few years ago. Early in the book, I stopped at a line describing Mrs. Bennet, the piece-of-work mother of the novel's heroine, Elizabeth, and her four sisters. It read, "When she was discontented, she fancied herself nervous." The sentence got me thinking about how often teens come to my office sharing that they feel anxious, but then go on to describe a frustrating fight with a friend or, with more than a hint of excitement in their voices, an upcoming playoff game that they'll be competing in. Often, when teens report feeling *anxious,* they seem to be saying that they feel stirred up, that they *don't feel calm.* Anxiety is certainly one form of emotional arousal—the one that psychologists link to feeling frightened or threatened—but it's also just one of a great number of emotions in the "not calm" category.

Today's teenagers use the term "anxiety" a lot. When I hear them use it in my office, I prick up my ears and listen for a chance to help them improve their emotional granularity. Keeping my mental thesaurus at the ready, I ask them to tell me more about what's going on. If a teenager describes a situation that has left them feeling scared or threatened, in my head I'll agree that the term "anxiety" fits and turn our work toward managing the teen's nerves. But once I get more of the story, it's not at all un-usual for my response to fall along the lines of "I hear that you feel anxious about your fight with your friend, which makes sense. But do you think you might also be feeling annoyed or ir-ritated by it?" or "There's no question that big games can be anxiety-provoking, but I'm wondering if you might also have some apprehension or even excitement about how it will go."

What I do in my office to refine the specificity of how teens describe their inner worlds, you can do at home. When teenagers talk about feeling anxious—or "upset," "pissed," "bummed," or any other vaguely defined emotion—they are usually handing us opportunities to help them develop their emotional vocabulary. If your son makes a sweeping statement, such as "Everything sucks!," try responding gently with "How come?" or "What's up?" Then listen for specifics. If he elaborates that "Our English teacher just dumped a truckload of homework on our class," em-pathize with the fact that he might now be feeling aggravated, or swamped, or beleaguered, or discouraged, or any other adjective that you think might hit the mark more closely. If your daughter shares that she's "not happy" about the cancellation of a long-anticipated event, let her know that it makes all the sense in the world for her to feel unhappy, but that it would be totally understandable if she also felt disappointed, let down, crushed, or resentful.

Offering teenagers subtler and pinpointed terms to describe their inner worlds supports them across two fronts: It turns the road to emotional relief through verbalization into a superhighway, and it's also a profound gesture of empathy. Bringing a teen's fuzzy description of psychological turmoil into focus with exact and accurate terms requires a real emotional investment and a high level of psychological attunement—a degree of devotion that most teenagers find greatly comforting.

## Getting Teens to Open Up

So far, this chapter has quietly assumed that teens will be given to talking about their emotions. But that's a pretty big assumption. What about the teens who are extremely private, the ones who rarely or never offer us an internal weather report even when we can see that a squall is brewing? Or what about teens who have language or learning differences that make it challenging for them to put their thoughts and feelings into words? Many parents raising teens who tend to keep their feelings to themselves spend a lot of time *wishing* they knew more about what their adolescent is thinking and feeling. They would jump at the chance to listen, headline, empathize, and help their teens refine their emotional vocabulary. Most would even welcome complaining! Instead, they often get conversations that go something like this:

"How was school?"

"Fine."

"Anything interesting happen today?"

"Nope."

Is there any way to overcome this reticence? It's not always easy to get teens talking about closely held emotions, but there are some strategies to up the odds of having a meaningful conversation. The first thing to remember is that teenagers, especially tight-lipped ones, *really* don't like to be put on the spot. So your number one priority is to keep your teen out of the hot seat.

One way is to steer clear of direct questions. Instead of asking "How do you feel about your new coach?" you can take an indirect tack: "What are people saying about the coach who just came in? Do they like her?" Instead of "Were you glad to hear that finals are now being held before winter break?" try "What's the word on the street about the new finals schedule?" Though we'd certainly prefer to know what our own teenagers feel about a given situation, consider it a win—especially with teens who tend to be quiet—to get a discussion going about any emotional topics that they might be willing to comment on. While our ultimate aim is to help teenagers find emotional relief by describing their own feelings, getting them to talk about what their peers are feeling might help get the ball rolling.

You can also stack the conversational deck in your favor by saving your questions for times when you and your teen are not face-to-face. Many parents find that they have some of their most unguarded discussions with their teenagers when they're together on a drive or a walk. It can be a lot easier for teenagers to share their inner world when they don't have to look at us. Whenever I want to bring up a delicate topic with one of my daughters, I wait until we're out driving, and *then* I wait until we're about three minutes from arriving back home. The combined effect of our both being eyes front and my daughter's knowing that the subject cannot possibly be entertained for long gives us a fighting chance for a meaningful, if brief, conversation that would otherwise be a nonstarter.

Another way to keep teens clear of the hot seat is to appreciate that the abstract nature of emotions makes them especially challenging to talk about. To ask questions about facts and events, such as "Did you have art class today?," is one thing. To inquire about the subtleties of a teen's emotional world is an entirely different ballgame. You may pitch a question like "You seem upset, what's going on?" and then be instantly ready, glove open and on your toes, to field the answer. But your teen may need time to process the question before swinging. This lag may also be influenced by your teen's thinking style—how much they like to talk through their thoughts as they take shape versus how much they like to fully work them out in their head before they speak. On top of that, there's the issue of processing speed—the pace at which people think—which varies widely from person to person and is not, incidentally, closely related to overall intelligence. With all these factors in play, you can see what a long shot it might be to ask your teen about a nebulous emotional experience she may be having and then get a prompt, satisfying reply. To account for teens who need time to think about what they're feeling, put some space between your question and their answer. "You've seemed out of sorts the last couple of days," you might say to your teen on a Saturday morning. "If you want to chat at any point this weekend, you know I'm always game."

Looking for yet one more way to keep teens out of the hot seat and make it easier for them to express their emotions more freely? Try reaching out by text. I was first put on to this approach by a friend, the mother of two adolescent boys who both hold their cards close to their chest. She shared with me that her deepest and most heartfelt conversations with her sons have inevitably occurred through text messages. Once, when one of her sons had ended the semester with uncharacteristically low grades in two of his classes, my friend and her husband tried to talk with him about what had happened. He kept telling them that he didn't know what to say, so they went to bed having given up on trying to have a conversation about it.

"After he went to school the next morning," my friend told me, "I texted him to say that he wasn't in trouble, but that we just wanted to make sense of his grades. He replied with the longest text I've ever gotten from anyone." In it, he said that he felt ashamed about the grades, terrible about disappointing them, and scared that they were mad at him. My friend and her son then texted back and forth over the day and were able to unpack the issue in a way that would never have been possible in person. "After all that, he texted me to say that he really appreciated our support and that he loves us. I burst into tears when I read it." A bit sheepishly, my friend added, "I just wish that he could say all this in person."

I saw no reason for my friend to feel self-conscious about the story. While it's easy to imagine that other parents are sitting around their kitchen table having long heart-to-hearts with their teenagers, I suspect that's pretty rare. I told her as much, and that I thought that she'd struck upon a brilliant solution, which I hoped that lots of other parents were already on to as well.

If we think about it, addressing emotionally charged topics by text is a perfect way to get a touchy conversation going while keeping teens out of the hot seat. They don't have to look at us, they can take as long as they need to answer, and the written response may result in a far more precise accounting of how they feel than they would ever communicate in person.

The next time your loath-to-talk teen leaves for school under an emotional cloud, try sending a text: "It seems as if you had a hard morning, how are you doing now?" If you get a meaningful response, jackpot—well done! By all means, text back a validating reply. But I'd urge you to resist the temptation to try to pick up the conversational thread in person at the end of the day. Switching from texting to talking might leave your teenager regretting having opened up and might cause both lines to go dead.

And if you get little or nothing back, don't despair. Teens, in my experience, *do* want to share what's on their mind with their parents. But they usually want to engage on their terms, not ours.

## Letting Teens Set the Terms of Engagement

Not long ago I visited a school in New Orleans, where I presented to the students, staff, and faculty during the day and to the parents in the evening. A heavy rainstorm started about an hour before the parents' talk, so the audience was a small but intrepid group who had arrived in full foul-weather gear. In that evening presentation I mentioned how much more forthcoming teens can be when we save our questions for the car. Once the talk was over and we had done the question-and-answer session, most of the parents headed back out into the storm, but a handful clustered near the podium to talk with me and catch up with one another.

A middle-aged man and his wife graciously thanked me for my presentation and wanted to talk further.

"What you said about teenagers being more talkative in the car?" he began. "That's true. At least that's what we find with our fourteen-year-old daughter. But the other time that she talks a lot is at night. When we're in bed reading and about to go to sleep, she comes into our room and plants herself in a chair. And then she'll talk to us for twenty minutes or so about all sorts of things."

His wife put her hand on his arm and was quick to say more.

"He used to try to shut this down because of the hour, telling her that it was getting late and we all needed to go to sleep. But I made him stop," she said, her husband now nodding in agreement. "She doesn't talk much otherwise, so we'll take what we can get."

A tall dad, a friend of theirs, was standing nearby listening to our conversation. As he heard them describing their daughter's practice of opening up at night, the look on his face shifted abruptly from mild interest to startled recognition. "That's exactly what I used to do when I was a teenager!" he interjected. "I would come home from boarding school and not say much to my parents until they were already in bed. Then I'd stand in their doorway, leaning against the doorframe, and tell them all about what had been happening at school. I hadn't thought about that until just now."

"This is truly fascinating!" I said to all three parents. Then, directing my question to the tall dad, I asked, "Do you think it was because you could end the conversation when you wanted to? That you could walk away knowing that your folks weren't going to get out of bed to ask you follow-up questions?"

"Yes, looking back on it, I think that's exactly what was going on," he said. I could see from their faces that this idea was dawning on the parents of the fourteen-year-old, too.

"Now that you say it," said the mom, "it seems like that's what's happening in our house as well. The conversation's over when our daughter decides it's over. Knowing her, I bet that makes it easier for her to open up."

So often, our efforts to get teenagers to share what's on their mind involve trying to engage them at the times and around the topics that make the most sense to us. Of course there's nothing wrong with greeting our teens at the end of the day with a friendly "How was school?" But we should be prepared for that conversation to go nowhere. Why? Because teenagers, at their very core, are autonomy-seeking creatures. When we ask a teenager about his day at a moment that works for us, we are in effect calling him to a meeting for which we ourselves have set both the time and the agenda. Given the strength of their drive for self-determination, I've learned that adolescents, especially sphinx-like ones, are most likely to open up when *they* get to set the terms of engagement. Through this lens, the nighttime chattiness that I learned about in New Orleans makes even more sense. In both cases, it was the teenager who was deciding when the meeting began and when it ended. And they were also the ones setting the agenda, calling the meeting only when their parents had already put their own agendas away for the day.

"Now wait a minute," you might be thinking, "should my teen really get to be the one who calls all the meetings? And is he supposed to be allowed to call them at odd hours? He knows that we love him and are curious about his life—isn't it reasonable to suppose that he could meet us halfway, being open to chat sometimes on his terms, sometimes on ours?" In truth, teenagers often meet us halfway, and we should bear as much in mind. Every time I get a real answer when I ask one of my daughters how she feels about school, her weekend plans, or anything else, she has agreed to my terms of engagement. She has set aside her marrow-deep wish to be in sole charge of her ship and has allowed me to board and inspect it.

As parents, we want our teens to steer our way when they need someone to talk to. This means that we need to stand ready to connect under terms that may work better for them than they do for us. Let's not blow it. Let's not shut down their odd-hour overtures without considering that this may be how they can express closely held emotions without sacrificing a sense of autonomy. Of course, this doesn't mean that you need to take midnight phone calls from your college student for nonemergency conversations. But it does mean that we should make room for the adolescent need for self-determination in how they go about sharing themselves with us. The same teen who stays at a distance during the day may pull up close at night. When this happens, let's remember that we're being called to a meeting we want to attend.

## Taking and Making Conversational Openings

Research shows that most adolescents like their parents and want to connect with us. In fact, a complaint that I often hear from teens is that when they *do* want to talk—even during normal business hours—it can be hard to get our attention. Whenever an adolescent brings this up in our clinical work, I can't help but sit in my office chair and feel guilty as I picture how these interactions play out in my own home.

For instance, without consciously meaning to have done so, I've designated dinner as the time when we'll get together and talk about the important aspects of our day. My daughters may oblige and participate in my agenda for our dinner meeting, or they may not be in the mood to talk at that time. Regardless, once the meal is cleaned up, I move on to the rest of my evening plans. I call my parents or my friends, dig out from under my email, work on my grocery list, and so on. At some point after dinner, with me in the middle of trying to figure out which items in the to-be-dealt-with pile on the kitchen counter can no longer be ignored, one of my girls stops by to say, "There was a fight at school today." I might turn toward her, nod, and even say "Whoa!"—but there's a good chance I'll miss her invitation to have a talk. Instead of setting the papers aside, tuning in, and asking some questions, I might only half listen to the rest of what she volunteers, trying mainly to hold on to my previous train of thought. I'm not proud of any of this, especially given that my daughters know me better than I know myself (just as your teen knows you) and can tell when my attention is divided.

There are certainly times when we shouldn't interrupt what we're doing. But if we're home and one of our teenagers wants to talk to us, we should recognize the opportunity for what it is and welcome it. My instincts in this department are not always good— there's little I enjoy more than checking tasks off my to-do list— but my decades of clinical practice have been a great help. For many years before I became the mother of teenagers, I heard the parents in my practice lamenting how quickly the end of high school had arrived. So whenever I feel torn between sticking with my own plan for the evening and setting it aside to engage, I remind myself that I will soon have evening upon evening to spend as I please. And when that time comes, I'll regret it if I didn't make the most of the nights when one of my teenagers was feeling chatty.

In addition to picking up the conversational topics that our kids put on the table, there's another way we can make it more likely that our teens will seek us out as a listening ear: by being around. Though we usually spend a lot of time with our children when they're younger, we see our kids less as they age. Normally developing teenagers tend to be busy with pursuits related to school, extracurriculars, jobs, friends, or all of the above. And many parents, myself included, welcome the freedom of being able to make plans without having to hire a babysitter. Just as the adolescents in my care sometimes complain that their parents don't always listen, many have also told me that they wish their parents were around more. Until I heard this grievance from enough teenagers to appreciate how common it was, it baffled me for two reasons. First, our teens often give us the impression that they'd *love it* if we weren't home so much. Second, I strongly suspected that the teenagers who were telling me that they wished their parents were around more were also ignoring those same parents most of the time when they *were* home.

Over time, however, I have come to think that teenagers feel most at ease when they know where their folks are, in much the same way that securely attached toddlers keep track of their parents' movements around the house even as they pursue their own activities. Further, having us nearby means that teenagers can readily talk with us about the topics they care about when, for them, the moment strikes.

So how do we make ourselves enough of a presence to be accessible to our teens, but not so much that we seem as if we're hovering? One friend of mine has agreed to his teenage daughter's request for him to work or read nearby while she does her homework. Another makes a practice of folding laundry each evening in the room where her teenagers watch TV. For my part, I save my customarily drawn-out kitchen cleaning for times I know my girls are going to be home. In this way, I am available, utterly interruptible, and right in their traffic pattern, just in case they have a sudden urge to talk.

## Owning and Repairing Parenting Mistakes

Wanting our kids to talk to us and going out of our way to make that possible doesn't mean we'll always get it right when they do. I was reminded of this one Tuesday after Thanksgiving when fourteen-year-old Corey arrived at our weekly appointment as angry as I'd ever seen her. She was so wound up that she didn't even unzip her parka when she came in and plunked herself down on my couch. Sitting stiffly upright, it was as if she hoped that keeping her coat fully zipped would help her to hold herself together.

"Is something up?" I asked, eager to find out what was going on.

"Arrgh!" she grunted through clenched teeth. "Thanksgiving was the worst!"

"What happened?"

She paused, took a wind-up breath, and poured out her complaint. "My aunt—my mom's sister—lives in Nashville, and she came up to have Thanksgiving with us. We were all having a good time—Thanksgiving is my favorite holiday—and I usually really like having my aunt around. But then after dinner we were cleaning up in the kitchen and she asked me how things were going with Reza, this boy in my class that I've had a crush on for forever."

I could see where this was headed.

"*I* didn't tell her about Reza—my mom did. I couldn't believe it! I played it off with my aunt—I was like, 'Oh, he's fine'—and she got it that I didn't want to talk about it. But I am *so* pissed at my mom."

"I see," I said. "Did you say something to your mom about it?"

"No. I mean she knows I'm mad, but I don't think she thinks it's a big deal," she said, finally unzipping her coat and letting her back relax into the seat.

"But clearly it is," I offered sympathetically.

"Yes! I can't believe that my mom told her about it. I feel like I can't have anything private."

"Do you think you will bring it up with your mom? That you'll let her know how mad you are?"

"Probably not," she said, "but I can tell you that's the last time I'm talking with her about anything I really care about."

Parents make mistakes. And an easy one to make is to share information that to us seems ordinary, unremarkable, even endearing, but to our teenager is meant to be like a state secret. Errors like this can keep our teens from wanting to express their emotions to us. Suppose you've already tried everything that this chapter has suggested to help teens open up—you've kept them out of the hot seat, let them set the terms of engagement, tuned in when they *are* in the mood to talk, and are as available as you can be should those moments arise—and your teen still hesitates to share anything of personal importance with you. At this point, it's worth considering carefully whether you might have said or done something that closed down the lines of communication.

If you suspect that you're in a situation like Corey's mom's—that you shared information that was meant to be kept private—offer your teen a genuine apology. Do this both because it is warranted and also as a way to try to reboot your connection to your teen and regain trust. As for effective apologies, researchers have found that they include six components: explicitly saying that you are sorry, offering an explanation, acknowledging responsibility, promising not to repeat the mistake, trying to make amends, and requesting forgiveness. If we were to script such an apology for Corey's mom, it would go something like this: "I'm sorry I told my sister about Reza, I didn't think you'd mind her knowing. But I realize now that that information was not mine to pass along. Going forward, I promise to keep our conversations between us unless I've gotten your permission to share something. I know I screwed this up and hope you might forgive me."

The following week, Corey arrived for her appointment far more at ease. She was talkative as usual and returned to the topic that had brought her to my practice in the first place—her difficulty making and keeping friends. As she shared the good news that over the weekend she'd gotten together with a girl she enjoyed spending time with in art class, I wondered whether I should double back to our conversation from the previous week. On the one hand, I'm always inclined to follow my clients' lead on how they want to use their time in therapy. On the other, it can seem insensitive or inattentive *not* to mention a previous week's session when it included an intense, and as yet unresolved, topic.

When Corey came to a stopping place, I let her know that I was glad to hear that she'd made a promising connection. Then I paused a moment before commenting, "Last week, you were pretty bothered about things with your mom."

"Oh, yeah," she said matter-of-factly, "they're better now."

"How come?" I asked.

"She could tell I was still upset about the Reza thing, so she brought it up. We talked about it and I let her know that I wasn't okay with her telling her sister the things I told her. My mom acted a little defensive, but she got it. So . . . I think we're good."

It didn't sound as though Corey got the full six-step apology that I generally recommend, but I also knew that she and her mom—who had been raising Corey on her own for nearly ten years—had a strong connection, which, I trust, helped them ride out this particular bump in their relational road.

Whether or not you have "blabbed" (as some teenagers say), I think that it's a good policy to let teens know that what they share with us will stay with us. Adolescents can collect a lot of emotionally freighted information in the course of a regular day. Knowing that they can unload details freely at home can be a weight off their mind and, as an added bonus, help them refrain from engaging in unnecessary gossip with their peers.

Of course, there may be times when your teenager shares information that must be disclosed, such as news of a friend who keeps getting blackout drunk or of a coach whose behavior is out of line. When these tricky situations arise, it's important to suppress the impulse to pick up the phone and make an informational end run around your teen. That would almost certainly leave your teenager regretting having opened up. Barring an immediate safety concern, work *with* your teen to figure out how to get the information where it needs to go.

Remember Zach? The sophomore who lost himself in a videogame when Mara, the girl he'd been making out with, asked him about the status of their relationship? He and I continued to work together through his junior year, and over that time he and Mara started to date in a serious way. As they became closer, Mara shared with him that she sometimes had thoughts about suicide but that she didn't believe she'd ever act on them. Zach was understandably unsettled by this revelation, and after several sleepless nights, he told his mom what had been keeping him awake. Zach's mom wanted to call Mara's parents right away, but Zach didn't want Mara to know he'd betrayed her confidence. Unsure what to do, Zach texted me to see if I could help them figure out a solution, so he and his mom and I got on a three-way call.

Once they brought me up to speed, I told Zach that I agreed that Mara's parents needed to know but added that, as I saw it, there was more than one way to make that happen. One route would be for Zach to tell Mara that he cared about her and wanted to help her to get the support she deserved. For that to happen, she'd need to tell her parents what she had told Zach, and if she couldn't, Zach would have to reach out to them himself. Another route would be for Zach or his mom to go ahead and call Mara's parents. After we talked it through, Zach wanted to go with the first approach, and when we met the following week, he shared what had happened.

"Mara didn't really want to say anything to her parents, but she knew it was the right thing to do. She told me that she'd tell them." He said that even though he trusted her, he told Mara that he'd be able to sleep better if her folks confirmed that she'd spoken to them. "She understood. Not too long after we talked, her dad sent me a text saying that he really appreciated that I'd helped Mara open up to them." While it's certainly quicker to make an impulsive phone call than to work with our teen on how to handle sensitive information, doing so comes with the risk of making teenagers clam up. Being patient and weighing other options can allow us to do the right thing without closing down the lines of communication at home.

Being too free with information teens share with us isn't the only error that can keep them from telling us what's really on their mind. Adolescents sometimes stop talking because we've reacted to their hurt feelings with judgmental commentary, perhaps responding to a teenager who is aching over having been left out, once again, by a longtime friend with "Why do you even hang out with Jack when you know that he'll ditch you in a heartbeat?" And they're likely to keep things to themselves if they have reason to think we'll come back at them with any version of "I told you so." If a teenager is angry with himself for not being able to afford the new sneakers he wants, reminding him that you thought he paid too much for the last pair might be a true, but unhelpful, response.

When your teen shuts down and you know where you went wrong, offer a heartfelt (full six-part!) apology. If you suspect you made a misstep somewhere along the line but don't know exactly what it was, try not to be defensive, and instead make an earnest appeal to your teen along these lines: "I can tell that you're not feeling comfortable talking with me about topics that are close to your heart. Is there anything I've done or said that has gotten in the way? I'm asking because I want to make it right between us."

## Valuing Nonverbal Expression

In October of my older daughter's senior year of high school, I walked into the kitchen to find her vigorously shaking an unopened can of seltzer water.

"*What* are you doing?" I asked, totally perplexed.

"The college process," she responded in a strained tone, continuing to shake the can as hard as she could, "is making me *so* tense! I'm going to get rid of some stress by spraying seltzer water all over the backyard!"

I love teenagers. To the problem of finding an outlet for their feelings, they come up with solutions—often very inventive ones—that would never occur to adults. Though my daughter's impromptu pressure valve for the stress of the college admissions season was a new one on me, I had no problem with it. With near anthropological interest I watched her spray seltzer on our grass and driveway, then come back in the house and return to working on her application essays.

What did I make of my daughter's mental health during that episode? First check: Did her feelings fit the moment? Amid the demanding, tedious, consequential, capricious college process, stress was a *perfectly* fitting response. Now, second check: Was she managing it effectively? As idiosyncratic as my daughter's emotional regulation tactic was, it still ticked the "effective" box. Why? Because teenagers are managing emotions well whenever they turn to adaptive strategies, meaning actions that provide relief without doing harm.

So far, this chapter has focused on helping teens *talk* about what they are feeling. While verbalization is a common and highly effective way to express emotions, it's hardly the only healthy or adaptive one. If your teenager just isn't a talker, or struggles to put thoughts and feelings into words, you're probably glad to hear this. And you may already be aware of the nonverbal tactics your teen uses to find an outlet for emotional tension.

Some teenagers take the edge off unpleasant feelings by channeling them into physical activity. When they become angry or irritated, they might go for a run, join a knock-around pickup basketball game, or practice a smashing tennis serve. Others find relief for unwanted feelings by turning to creative outlets. They might make drawings that communicate a sense of longing, write stories or poems centered on themes of disappointment, pound out a song on the piano to release frustration, or belt out a tune to vent indignation. As one talented teenage musician explained to me, when his mom asks how he's feeling, "My mind just fills with static, but when I'm writing lyrics, that's how I figure out what's happening in my head."

Not all teenagers create their own music, but experience has taught me that a huge percentage of them *listen* to music as a way to manage their feelings. I have my own vivid memories of listening to particular songs when in particular moods as a teenager, and I'm guessing that you have these memories too. These days, when I speak to high school audiences about coping with stress, anxiety, and other toll-taking emotions, I always set aside time to ask how many of them listen to playlists they've created for when they want to shake off a bad mood. Usually, almost every hand goes up. Then I ask my audience to raise their hand if they have made a playlist dedicated to any of several emotional categories, which I call off one by one. It turns out that lots of teenagers have "happy," "pump-up," and "chill" playlists. But even more have "angry" and "sad" playlists.

Given the incredible power that music has to shape how we feel, it might seem strange that so many teens would make playlists for *bad* moods. But they do. Just as we, with our prehistoric mixtapes, did when we were teenagers. How come? Because adolescents have an intuitive grasp of one of my favorite psychological maxims: When we're dealing with a painful feeling, often the only way out is through. Teenagers have told me, and research confirms, that when they are burdened by dark or unpleasant emotions, they'll sometimes listen to a song that matches their mood, with the express aim of using that music to activate the tears, angry one-teen dance party, or raucous sing-along that will help them bring down their discomfort.

While music generally helps teens ride out choppy emotional waters, some adults may worry that listening to emotionally intense songs—especially forceful and edgy music, such as heavy metal—may actually increase distress rather than reduce it. One of my favorite research studies addresses this very question. Psychologists recruited a group of adolescents who enjoyed listening to one or more forms of "extreme" music, a category that included heavy metal, punk, screamo, and hardcore. Electrodes attached to the teenagers monitored their heart rate as—at the instruction of the research team—they gave detailed descriptions of an experience that had made them irate, a technique that has been found to effectively stir up feelings of anger. Half of the research participants then listened to ten minutes of music from one of their own extreme music playlists, while the other half sat in silence. After telling their stories, and then again after the ten minutes of either listening to music or sitting in silence, participants filled out forms asking them to rate their emotional state "at that moment."

What did the researchers find? For everyone in the study, recalling the experience that made them angry led to an increase in heart rate (a measure of emotional arousal) and self-reported feelings of hostility, irritability, and stress. And, regardless of whether they spent the next ten minutes listening to their extreme music or sitting quietly, *all* of the research participants reported that their feelings had cooled. But here's where the two groups differed. For those adolescents who spent the ten minutes listening to extreme music, their heart rate remained elevated but did not increase. For those who sat silently for the ten minutes, their heart rate slowed. In what may be the study's most interesting finding, after the ten minutes, the research participants who listened to extreme music playlists reported an increase in *positive* emotions—they felt energized and inspired—while those who sat silently reported no increase in positive feelings.

The takeaways for this study are many. First, it dispels the notion that extreme music makes angry teenagers angrier. Everyone in the study reported that they felt calmer ten minutes after riling themselves up, whether they had listened to extreme music or not. Second, while the music listeners' heart rates remained elevated, they *did not increase,* providing physiological evidence that they did not become angrier as a result of listening to intense music. Third, the fact that the music listeners' heart rates remained elevated as they went from telling their ire-provoking stories to hearing their playlists suggests that the intense music allowed the participants to prolong—and more fully experience—the physiological arousal associated with getting mad.

Now, you may be thinking that it sounds like a *bad* thing for teenagers to prolong their anger. Let me explain. In the end, the researchers found that being able to really "get into" the experience of feeling mad helped the music listeners *alone* turn the corner, with the negative emotions of hostility, irritation, and stress giving way to the positive emotions of feeling energized and inspired. In other words, the immersive emotional experience of listening to music seemed to speed the adolescents in the study through—and out the other side of—their negative emotions. Though this study focused on anger and extreme music, other research has found that when teenagers are sad and listen to melancholy music, there is a similar benefit. In finding an outlet for their sorrow, they hasten a sense of relief.

• • •

To return to now familiar terrain: Experiencing psychological pain is an unavoidable aspect of life and—given the many normal challenges and disappointments inherent to adolescence—an inescapable fact of being a teenager. As such, our goal cannot be to prevent or chase away adolescent distress but rather to help our teenagers *regulate* their emotions. This means, in part, ensuring that they find healthy outlets for the uncomfortable ones. Adolescents often intuitively do this on their own, perhaps by talking about their inner world, but also by jumping on trampolines, spraying seltzer in the backyard, beating their drum sets, listening to carefully curated playlists, and more.

Around these nonverbal expressions of emotion, adults have two jobs. One is to recognize and accept that teens sometimes use quirky but adaptive tactics to get their feelings out; behavior that appears inexplicable at first glance may turn out to make good emotional sense for our kid. The other is to actively support their inventive approaches, no matter how offbeat they may seem to us; if your teen's getting much-needed relief costs you only a can of seltzer water and a wet driveway, treat it as a bargain.

## Recognizing Unhealthy Emotional Expression

What about emotional expression that causes harm either to your teenager or to someone else? Sometimes a teen comes home from school in a rotten mood and takes out his frustration—either physically or verbally—on an unsuspecting younger sibling who happens to be in the wrong place at the wrong time. Sometimes angry teenagers will say hurtful things to people they care about. When anything like this happens, it should always be taken seriously. The teenager's emotions may be entirely justified, but the way those emotions are being expressed is a problem. As the adults on the scene, we'll want to help teens learn to see this critical distinction. "I get it that you had a hard day," you can say, "but attacking your sister isn't how to deal with it. You can tell me what's wrong, go for a run, or find some other way to feel better. Just leave your sister out of it." Or "It's okay to be pissed, but you can't speak to me like that. Let's talk when you've had a chance to calm down."

Even when teenagers attribute their hurtful behavior to emotions that garner our sympathy—such as when they chalk up being short-tempered to feeling anxious or stressed—we shouldn't give them a free pass. "If you want to talk about what's making you anxious, I'm here for that," you could offer, "but being cranky with me is only going to leave us both feeling worse." If you sometimes need to redirect your teenager's emotional expression, you are hardly alone—it's fair to say that this challenge just comes with the territory of raising adolescents. So long as teens dependably find their way to harmless outlets for their feelings, there's no reason for alarm, even if they do need reminders from time to time. If, however, your teen seems stuck in a rut and cannot move beyond expressing emotion in ways that might bring fleeting relief but hurt others or strain important relationships, consult with a mental health professional for guidance and support.

Sometimes teens discharge their emotions in ways that are, without question, real grounds for concern. We noted in chapter 2 that boys, in particular, are sometimes socialized to deal with distress through aggression or violence, though this is hardly exclusive to males. Also, adolescents sometimes relieve emotional discomfort by hurting *themselves*, such as when they engage in cutting or other forms of self-harm.

Whether the violence is directed outward or inward, there are key points to keep in mind. First, teenagers who are hurting others or themselves are letting us know that they are suffering and that they don't have healthy ways to express that suffering. Second, teenagers who rely on violence warrant help, regardless of who is being harmed. This should come in the form of professional guidance, so that they can come to understand what's behind their destructive behavior and develop healthy strategies for gaining emotional relief.

Finally, the *magnitude* of emotional expression should not interfere with aspects of a young person's life that are essential to growth and development. Teens will sometimes feel nervous, but that nervousness should not be so acutely or persistently expressed that it gets in the way of going to school, spending time with peers, or doing other things they ought to be doing. Teens will sometimes feel angry, but their expression of anger should not be so powerful or pervasive that it hamstrings them from making or keeping friends. Teens will sometimes feel sad, but the expression of sadness should not sweep aside their ability to be hopeful, happy, or productive. If this is happening, it's time to seek a professional evaluation, as the teen may be suffering from an anxiety disorder, mood disorder, or something else.

When teenagers feel their emotional waters rising, they need to be able to channel them into adaptive forms of expression. Adolescents may have good instincts for how to do this, but the deliberate support of loving adults makes a great difference in helping teens develop their ability to express their feelings well.

In addition to expression, there is another side to emotional self-management: the ability to bring feelings under control as needed. To that, let's now turn our attention.

■ ■ ■ ■ ■

## CHAPTER FIVE

# Managing Emotions, Part Two: Helping Teens Regain Emotional Control

At 8:59 on a Monday morning, my phone rang with a number I didn't recognize. When I don't know who's at the other end of the line, I usually let a call roll to voicemail. But I happened to be free, so I picked up.

"Oh! Dr. Damour," said a man who clearly expected to be leaving a message. "I'm glad I got you. This is Mark, Anna's dad—you met with us last year when Anna was thirteen."

"Yes, I remember you," I said, recalling that Mark and his wife, Rachel, had visited my office when Anna was at the unpleasant height of the separation-individuation process, insisting that her mom change out of her "dumpy" outfit before her friends came over, and the like. "How are you? And what's going on?"

"Well, we're okay," he said genially. "Of course, I wouldn't be calling if *everything* was fine . . ."

"Well, I suppose that's true," I said lightheartedly.

"But mostly things are good. Anna's generally in a much better place than when we met with you. And things unfolded the way you said they would. She ended up getting really serious about her robotics team, and that, plus starting high school and finding a solid group of friends, made a big difference. Anna's done a great job of starting to figure out what she's all about, and she seems to be more comfortable all around. For the most part, she's a lot of fun these days."

"I'm so glad to hear it. Thirteen can be a challenging age, but with teenagers it's usually true that nothing stays the same for too long."

"But something new has come up," he said, "and Rachel and I don't know what to do. Anna now gets really preoccupied with worries that someone she loves will die, and she can't seem to get past them. She tells us that she's afraid something bad will happen to me, or to her mom, or to someone else she cares about. Nothing we do or say seems to help. Can we set up a time to come in?"

"Absolutely," I said. "How does Thursday look for you?"

Later that week Mark and Rachel sat next to each other on my couch, now with a very different concern from the one that brought them my way the year before.

"We've done everything we can think of," said Rachel. "We've been letting her talk about her fears, in hopes that seeing that we're not bothered by them will calm her down. We let her know that we understand how upsetting it is to realize that the people we love won't live forever. And we reassure her that we're taking good care of ourselves and that we plan to be around for a long time."

"It's actually awful to watch her be tortured by these concerns," added Mark. "I told her that if it's this painful for me to witness, it must be incredibly painful for her to be living with, and she said that it is. But when we encourage her to not think about it, or not think about it so much, she says that she tries to stop, but just can't."

"Did anything happen," I asked, "that seemed to bring these worries on? Was there a death, or has she been watching shows or reading books where someone dies?"

Rachel was quick to reply, "I had that same question! When I asked, Anna said that wasn't it—the worries just seemed to start out of the blue. We truly have no idea where all of this is coming from. But it's making her miserable, and the more she talks about it, the worse she seems to feel."

After pausing to consider it for a moment, I said, "I know that Anna recently turned fourteen, and one of the great things that happens right around that age is that normal changes in the brain lead to a surge in the capacity for abstract thinking. Mostly, this is wonderful. Fourteen-year-olds suddenly become much more insightful than ever before and can see the world from new perspectives. But it's also been my experience that the arrival of abstract thinking can bring with it some very unsettling existential concerns."

Having practiced for a long time now, I've learned that it's not unusual for teens to become pretty freaked out by this fresh dimension to their thinking. I've cared for other young teenagers who, like Anna, suddenly become alarmed by life's impermanence despite having long known about death. Or who find themselves unhappily preoccupied with profound philosophical questions, such as whether they have a right to enjoy themselves when there's so much suffering in the world. The advent of abstract thinking can even give rise to thoughts that run toward the surreal, as they did with a boy I treated who all but confessed in my office that he wondered if life was an elaborate charade, a big joke that everyone else but him was in on. And I have my own clear memory, from around age fourteen, of briefly wondering whether, instead of being a regular kid growing up in Denver, I might actually be a member of an extraterrestrial species who had accidently been dropped off on Earth and raised as a human.

Most of the time, teenagers can set aside or let go of such disconcerting existential questions (as I quickly did with my notion about being on the wrong planet), but occasionally they get stuck on them, as happened to Anna. Indeed, Anna's struggle here highlights a critical point about emotion regulation. Usually, expressing feelings confers sufficient relief. But when it doesn't, another approach is called for.

"Based on what you're telling me," I said to Rachel and Mark, "you've done everything right. You've encouraged Anna to talk about her fears; you've been compassionate, patient, and even sensitive to how miserable it must be for her to be hounded by these new worries. Letting teens talk about what's wrong usually helps them feel better. But when talking about emotions doesn't seem to provide comfort, then we need to try something else. Let's not aim for more expression, let's try to keep Anna's emotions from running wild and trampling on everything else."

## When Emotions Need to Be Brought Under Control

To recap, emotional regulation rests on a pair of complementary approaches: finding outlets for uncomfortable feelings and, when it's needed, finding ways to rein them in. The previous chapter was the playbook for helping teenagers *express their emotions* to get relief. This chapter is the playbook for helping adolescents *regain control of their emotions* when they start to get the better of them.

Before we dive into strategies that help teens wrangle their emotions as needed, there's a critical point that bears repeating: When responding to teens' psychological distress, we will almost always want to exhaust our options for helping them express their emotions *before* running any of the plays in this chapter. Rachel and Mark did this by talking with Anna about her worries and empathizing about how unsettling they were for her. They called me only when what they were doing wasn't helping.

Why do we need to give emotional expression a chance to work before we guide teenagers to corral their emotions instead? I'll give you four excellent reasons. First, finding a healthy outlet for uncomfortable feelings—discussing them, having a good cry, listening to sad or angry music, and so on—usually does the job, providing all the relief a teenager needs. Second, making ourselves available to talk with our teenagers about their ups and downs is one of the most enriching aspects of parenting, and it goes a long way toward strengthening our relationships with them. Third, demonstrating our loving interest in what's weighing on our teens models the attentive compassion that they should come to hold as a standard for all of their close relationships. Fourth, trying to implement any of the strategies offered in this chapter almost certainly won't work unless we have already given emotional expression a chance to work its magic.

Most parents, myself included, have learned this fourth point the hard way. A teen tells his mom he's nervous about an upcoming debate tournament, she gently suggests that he could help himself out by spending more time preparing his argument, and he storms off in a huff. Or a girl weepily complains to her dad about her massive history project, and he aptly notes that she's been staying up late and would probably feel better if she got more sleep, causing her to become even more distraught. In both scenarios, the parent's advice might be spot-on, but when our *first* response is to point out how they could curb their discomfort, teenagers often feel injured. Rather than accept our input as the sound and well-meaning guidance that it is, they tend to feel dismissed or invalidated. Accordingly, in this chapter we'll not only detail the many ways that adolescents can bring their emotions under control, we'll also need to consider how to introduce these strategies in such a way that our teenagers are more likely to give them a try.

So how do we know when it's time to point teenagers toward

*controlling* their emotions rather than *expressing* them? Here's a good rule of thumb: It's when expression isn't working, and feelings have become so intense or overwhelming that they are getting in the way of teens doing what they need or want to do. If your teen is cranky after a rough day at his job, refuses to talk about what's wrong, but is still able to tackle his homework and help clean up after dinner, you can stand back, let him be grumpy, and trust his troubles will resolve on their own. If, however, your teen wants to cancel an important interview because she is so afraid that she'll mess it up and talking about her worries isn't putting her mind at ease, it's time to help her get her fearful feelings back in their box.

There are many ways for teens to get the upper hand on disruptive emotions. Let's start by taking a close look at the benefits of distraction.

## Distraction—An Important Tool for Emotion Regulation

Usually when we talk about distraction, we treat it as a bad thing. And it certainly can be when it's time to focus on our work, a conversation, or the road on which we're driving. But distraction can at times be a simple, practical, and efficient way for teenagers to regulate their emotions. It's a tactic that they often turn to intuitively. Picture, for example, a teenager who has just arrived home from an especially exhausting day at school. Already feeling worn down, he starts unloading his backpack in order to take stock of his homework for the night. As his pile of assignments rises, so does his internal tide of agitation. The longer he looks at the work he needs to do, the more frustrated he becomes as he thinks about the evening ahead. Sensing that he may soon be flooded by resentment, he abruptly turns to his computer and searches for funny YouTube videos. As he watches one entertaining clip after another, his consternation ebbs away. Twenty minutes later, he closes his computer, returns to the pile of homework, and gets started on the first assignment.

It might seem strange to endorse a visit to YouTube as a wise strategy for emotion regulation. But let's consider the alternatives. What if the boy had allowed his distress to rise until it overwhelmed him and erupted as an angry outburst? Or what if he had an emotional meltdown from which he needed an hour to recover before he could return to his homework? Even working out his agitation by going for a long run, as fine an outlet for his discomfort as that may be, might not be a workable solution on this particular night, given that he doesn't have that kind of time. If—and I appreciate that this is a big if—teens can keep their distracting activities to short, relief-granting intervals, we should quietly admire how naturally, and often seamlessly, they swivel the spotlight of their attention in order to help themselves maintain their emotional equilibrium.

At times, emotionally overloaded teens would benefit from a dose of distraction but can't get there on their own because they are caught in an emotion with a very tight grip, as Anna was with her worry. That's when it's time for adults to step in.

"To be most helpful to Anna right now," I said to Rachel and Mark, "we'll want to see if you can help her switch her train of thought onto a new track."

"Okay," said Mark, "but I'm not sure we can; because she seems pretty stuck on this one."

"It will take some doing," I said, "and I think that the first step is to be direct with her about the fact that you are going to try something new and explain why. How would she take it if you told her that you had been hoping that talking about her concerns would make her feel better, but since that hasn't been the case, you want to come at it from a different angle?"

"I think she'd get it," said Rachel.

"From there, you can let her know that you want to see if she can get the worries to quiet down by focusing on them less."

"But we've already suggested that she try to stop thinking about them," Mark countered, "and she said that she can't."

"Right," I said, "but I think there's more we can do on that front. One option would be for you to talk with her about her mind being like a television, and that she can change her mental channel when her worries about death get going."

"How would she do that?" asked Rachel more than a little skeptically.

"You could talk her through what else she could think about—what other channels she could switch to. Perhaps she could make a list of her plans for the summer, sketch out ideas for how to redo her room, if she's into that kind of thing, or play an online game. If she has the time, she can also change her mental channel by getting lost in a good book or a movie that would keep her mind really busy."

"You suggested that that was *one* option," said Mark, "and I'm not sure it's one she'll go for. What else could we try?"

"Fair enough," I said. "You know Anna better than anyone else and will have the best sense of what will and won't work for her. Another option would be to set aside time for her to talk with you about her worries, but to have that time be planned and limited—perhaps ten minutes after dinner each night, or every other night if she'd go for that."

"This sounds more promising," said Rachel. "Are you suggesting that she'll be able to think about other things during the day if she knows that we've got a planned time for her to focus on her concerns?"

"Yes, that's exactly it. The point is to pull her thoughts away from what's upsetting her as much as possible by designating a specific, limited time for her to concentrate on them. And I think that you'd explain it to her in just that way: that you want her to save her thoughts about death for the planned time, and to think about other things outside of that time."

"That actually feels workable," said Mark, "because I do think that she'll feel a lot better if she can stop thinking about death so much. But we're not really getting to the bottom of where this is all coming from. Shouldn't we try to?"

"You're right," I said, "we're not. Though I'm usually in the business of helping teenagers explore, understand, and express their painful feelings, there are times when I make exceptions, and this is one of them. And with this particular kind of worry, I have found that once teenagers' ability to think abstractly stops being so new, their existential concerns usually ease up on their own. In the meantime, though, let's help Anna get a break from these fears."

They left my office agreeing to give our plan a try, and a month later Mark called with good news. "Anna's definitely doing better," he said. "She liked the idea of having a plan for *when* she'd talk about her worries so that she could mostly ignore them the rest of the time. At first, we kept to an every-night schedule, but then she said she didn't want to talk about her fears as often as that. In the last week, she's only brought them up once. I don't know if she's doing better because her nerves aren't so frayed, or if, as you said, she's just getting used to being able to think more deeply about all kinds of things. Either way, she seems more like her old self again."

Using distraction to push the pause button on distressing thoughts can go a long way toward helping adolescents keep their emotions from becoming overwhelming—and there's more to it than simply "not thinking about your feelings." In fact, there are a couple of subtler processes at work. First, stepping away from what's troubling them can give teenagers a chance to put it in perspective. As a high school sophomore once said to me, "Something can go wrong during the school day and I'll think about it nonstop. It will feel like the biggest deal in the world. Then I'll go to practice for a couple of hours and I'll be too busy to think about it for a while. Then when I remember the issue after practice, I'm not even sure why it bothered me so much." Second, locking in at length on a disconcerting feeling can elevate blood pressure and heart rate and dump stress hormones into the bloodstream. Finding something else to focus on can relax the body and give it a chance to recover from the taxing biological consequences of agonizing over a concern. Distraction can be an especially valuable way to reduce stress caused by a problem that has no easy solution.

When teenagers get stuck in painful psychological ruts and we think it might be useful for them to find another focus, there are steps we can take to increase the odds that such a suggestion will be well received. First, we should be sure, as Anna's parents were, that talking about the problem isn't helping before proposing distraction as a new strategy. Next, we should be transparent about *why* we are switching gears from encouraging discussion to encouraging distraction, a conversation that can begin along these lines: "Talking about this doesn't seem to be helping you feel better. Do you think it might be a good idea to take a break from thinking about it?" After that, we can make it clear that we are only pressing the pause button on the topic, not trying to end discussion of it altogether, and lay down a plan to return to the issue in a day or two to see if it looks any different. Helping teenagers break free of concerns that have hijacked their attention, even if only for a while, doesn't eliminate the source of their distress. But it can keep them from becoming emotionally over-whelmed.

## Small Pleasures, Big-Time Mood Control

We all seek ways to comfort ourselves when upset. After a tough day at work we might flop on the couch with a magazine, take a bubble bath, or have extra dessert. For teenagers, however, sooth-ing measures are especially helpful.

The neurological developments in the teenage brain cause adolescents to feel *everything* more acutely than the rest of us do. The uncomfortable feelings hit them harder, but fortunately, soothing activities also count for more. I have my own vivid memories of how much I enjoyed the sensation of driving on a winding road while listening to music when I was a teenager. I can still get a hint of that old bliss when I'm steering around a curve with a good song playing, but I know that such moments will never again lift my spirits the way they did when I was seven-teen. So, when your teenager is obviously uneasy but not in the mood to talk, don't underestimate the power of what can seem like small pleasures. Stand back and appreciate the peace that descends over your daughter as she gets a handle on her bad day by curling up under a blanket and enjoying a favorite cup of tea. Be confident that suggesting getting takeout from your son's fa-vorite restaurant might go a long way toward easing his disap-pointment about losing a class election. When we know that our teenagers are upset, our script may be for them to tell us all about what's wrong so that we can offer them our empathy, and per-haps our advice. But our teenagers' script—either because they're not in the mood to talk or because they sense that talking isn't the right fix—may be to drink some hot chocolate, take a quiet walk with the dog, or look at old pictures.

What any given teenager finds comforting will be highly personal. What works for one teen won't work for another. This is something I always bring up with large audiences of adolescents whenever I'm hoping to help each of them home in on their own preferred ways of coping with unwanted feelings. I always ask the group to give me a show of hands in response to two statements. "Raise your hand," I'll begin, "if, when something's really bothering you, cleaning up your room helps you feel better." Typically, about a third of the teens in the audience raise their hands. After they've put them down, I'll say, "Okay, now raise your hand if cleaning up your room is the *absolute last* thing you would do on a day when you're feeling lousy." A different third of them raise their hands. (The remaining third, I've always assumed, don't find much of a link between the state of their bedroom and their mood.)

So pay attention to what comforts *your* teenager. When feeling lousy, some teens take a long bath or shower, others doodle, meditate, bake or cook, play videogames, watch a favorite movie or TV show for the umpteenth time, or read. Listening to music is an especially popular choice for teens when they are in a bad mood. As we know from the previous chapter, they sometimes choose mood-*matching* songs to help catalyze the expression of anger or sadness when they're feeling mad or low; at other times, they choose mood-*countering* music—happy or upbeat songs—to help themselves feel better.

You've probably noticed that there's not always a clear line between distractions and comforts, and there certainly doesn't need to be. What matters is that we recognize that our teens often have great instincts for how to calm their own rough emotional waters, that we catch on to their go-to strategies, and that we put this knowledge to good use.

One of my friends observed that her son dealt with hard days by coming home and rolling around on the floor with the family dog. Knowing this, she made a point of bringing the dog along when she picked her son up from basketball practice on a day when she suspected he'd be getting into the car with the news that he hadn't made the team. We should be sure to honor teens' preferred approaches to soothing themselves even if, for example, they do things that we think have little value, such as playing with makeup. And if an unhappy teen doesn't want to talk or finds that it's not helping, consider asking, "Is there something that might help you feel better? Would you want to take a long shower?"

There's something else adults should be aware of when it comes to how teens choose to comfort themselves. Many of them find it soothing to engage in what I think of as emotional time travel. Mature and capable high school girls will sometimes re-center themselves by watching *The Lion King* or old Nickelodeon shows they loved when they were younger. Some boys who have been shaving for years still lose themselves in their *Captain Underpants* books when they need to shift emotional gears. Teens have explained to me that returning to *Mulan* or *Percy Jackson* transports them to a time of life that was much less stressful. Spending an hour or two revisiting a bygone phase when they were free from acne, final exams, or having to get a summer job can help teens find their feet and return to the demands of adolescence. If you come around the corner to discover your grown child sprawled out on the couch watching *Phineas and Ferb* in the same spot he claimed when he was seven, don't look at him askance. Rather, enjoy how inventively and effectively teenagers regain their mental equilibrium when they need to.

## Taking Sleep Seriously

Being a psychologist means that I often meet people at a horrible point in their lives. This was exactly what was about to happen as I walked to my waiting room to introduce myself to Jed, a high school senior who had come to see me because one of his best friends had recently been killed in a car accident. I had heard about this tragedy in our community before I received a message from Jed's mother, who was referred to me by his pediatrician. Her voicemail explained that once the initial shock of the news wore off, Jed "fell apart" and had been alternatingly numb, angry, and despondent. She also let me know that he was skeptical about therapy and had only begrudgingly agreed to meet with me.

As I walked out to meet them, I found Jed sitting beside his mom, his body angled forward, with his elbows resting on his knees and his hands clasped. Through the triangular window between his forearms, he stared at the floor. Without sitting up, he turned his head to acknowledge my entrance. "Hi," I said, "I'm Dr. Damour." As Jed's mother thanked me for meeting with her son, he languidly unfolded himself to his full height and, without saying a word, conveyed that he would follow me to my consulting room but only because he felt he had no choice.

Once the two of us were in my office, Jed continued to communicate a great deal while sizing me up silently. With his gaze alone he managed to say, "Lady, I don't know you at all. You cannot possibly think that it makes sense for me to share my raw pain and excruciating vulnerability with someone I met a minute ago." In truth, I felt that Jed was wordlessly making an excellent point. Therapy is a pretty strange arrangement. Adults who seek out counseling are willing to accept the premise that it can be helpful to share intimate thoughts and feelings with a well-trained stranger. Teenagers, though, can find this to be a pretty odd idea and aren't always on board.

Instead of waiting for Jed to decide to open up, I thought it was time for me to bring out a line that I learned from Duane Lee Chapman—a man better known as Dog the Bounty Hunter. If you are not familiar with Dog, he was the muscular, weather-beaten, blond-mullet-sporting star of a reality TV show that followed his exploits as he located and arrested bail jumpers. While I was flipping channels one night, I joined an episode as Dog knocked on a fugitive's door. When the door opened and Dog registered the look of surprise on his target's face, Dog calmly said, "Look. I don't know you, and you don't know me. But we have to leave here together," before going on to explain that they could do that the easy way or the hard way. I admired the ease and precision with which he acknowledged the strangeness of the situation, and I saw that for me, clinically, this approach would be appreciated by teenagers, who as a rule are allergic to interactions that seem fake or inauthentic.

Channeling Dog, I said gently to Jed, "Look. I don't know you, and you don't know me. But I know that your friend has died and I'm here to try to be of help." Jed's body relaxed, and the message on his face shifted. Now it read, "Okay, lady. I know *one* thing about you. You're not *totally* full of shit." I took this small opening to ask, "Do you want to talk about the accident, or would it be better for me to ask you some questions just to get to know you a bit?"

"You can ask me some questions," he said flatly.

So I asked Jed straightforward questions about where he went to school, the makeup of his family, whether he'd always lived in our area, and what he was planning to study in college. I stayed far away from the accident, waiting to see if he would bring it up, which eventually he did.

"I'm planning to major in engineering, which was Matty's plan too."

Knowing that Matty was the boy who had died, I nodded and softly responded, "I see." We then sat quietly together, something that I've become very comfortable with from years of being a practicing clinician. My ease with silence seems to help teens feel all right with it too. I hoped that showing Jed that I was not about to barge ahead with questions about the accident would help him feel safe to tell me more about it, which he then did. He talked about the flurry of texts he received when Matty's fatal accident happened, how he didn't believe it was true until it was confirmed by his school, how "nothing felt real" at the funeral, and the fact that now he "just couldn't feel right."

I followed along as he spoke and waited until he took a long pause before I said, "I am so sorry about Matty, and I am glad you are here, because you deserve a world of support. Can I ask you a question that will help us think about how to get you through this?"

"Sure."

"Are you able to sleep?"

Whenever someone comes to me in a crisis, I rely on this question to direct the next step of our work. When the answer is yes, I move toward helping clients process the crisis. When the answer is no, I prioritize helping my client get some sleep. Why is getting sleep necessary before turning to anything else? Because sleep is the glue that holds human beings together. Even in the absence of a tragedy, people who aren't sleeping soon find that they struggle to regulate their emotions. We probably know this from our own lives, and it has also been amply demonstrated by research. One study, for instance, asked parents to rate their teenagers' moods after five nights in a row of sleeping ten hours, and again after five nights in a row of sleeping six and a half hours. As one might expect, the sleep-deprived teenagers were more anxious, hostile, confused, irritable, and emotionally reactive.

Jed answered my question: "Actually, no. I'm having a really hard time at night. It's not even that I'm thinking about Matty all the time, I just can't seem to calm down enough to fall asleep."

"That's good to know, and it gives us a place to start. Because if you're not sleeping, you're going to feel lousy no matter what. Once you've gotten some sleep under your belt, then we can do a lot more to help you find your way through this."

From there I went through my tried-and-true list of strategies that can help teenagers fall and stay asleep. Jed liked to exercise and was open to increasing the intensity of his daily workouts, since upping exercise, I explained to him, has been found to improve sleep quality in both adolescents and adults. He knew that it wasn't helping him to be on his phone and computer late into the night, and he was tired enough to consider stepping away from them an hour or so before he meant to fall asleep. Jed didn't drink caffeine, so I skipped my usual recommendation of cutting that off by midday.

"Think of sleep not as a switch you can flip," I said, "but as a destination you arrive at after putting yourself on the path to it. If you want to go to sleep at eleven, you're going to need to get on that path, which means winding down tech, and anything else that could stir you up, by ten."

When teenagers become overwrought over small things or are unusually reactive or temperamental, we should look into the possibility that they are getting nowhere near the eight to ten hours of sleep (yes, you read that right, *eight to ten* hours) that adolescents need. Should you suspect that too little sleep is a likely culprit, you might lovingly say, "Honey, right now you seem to be held together with Scotch tape. I know that you've got a lot going on, and I'm wondering if part of what's making things hard is that you are very, very tired." Settle in for a conversation about the many demands on your teenager's time (which are certainly real) and be prepared to get creative about what can be skipped, paused, or canceled, at least for a little while, to make time for more sleep. For teens who resist—insisting that fatigue is not the problem, and if it is, caffeine is the answer—adults can see if they're willing to try an "experiment" in which they sleep more for just a couple of nights to see if that makes a difference. When teens are better rested, they are also better at reasoning. After a few full nights of sleep, with their tank full again, they may be able to recognize just how much sturdier they feel emotionally. From that point it becomes a lot easier to convince them that sleep needs to be a priority.

## Deliberate Breathing—Sounds Absurd, Works Great

When adolescents become overwhelmed by emotion—whether they are drowning in sadness or swamped by anxiety—one method that can help them get their head back above water is breathing deeply and slowly. This is a trusted technique used by professionals who do high-stress work, such as U.S. Navy SEALs. But if you try to tell a profoundly upset teenager that *taking deep breaths* will help him feel better, an eye roll may be the kindest response you'll get. Teenagers are naturally skeptical of advice that does not make intuitive sense, and there really is no obvious reason for them to believe that there's a link between their breathing patterns and what they're feeling in the moment. Even so, you can sell your teenager on this idea, but you'll have to explain the underlying science.

Whenever I find myself wanting to persuade an adolescent to consider that deliberate breathing can be a tactic for quickly regaining emotional control, I start by acknowledging that taking deep breaths to manage unruly feelings can sound far-fetched. This admission usually gets my foot in the door. From there I explain that though it sounds a little mystical, it's actually a biologically based intervention that allows us to tap into and control the workings of our own nervous system.

Our nervous system comprises two networks. First, there's the *sympathetic* network, which "sympathetically" responds to our moment-to-moment experiences. When we perceive a threat, the sympathetic network activates. The part of the brain that perceives threats has been around since we lived in caves and is not very discriminating. It regards almost any threat as if it's a tiger and thus directs the sympathetic network to mobilize our ancient fight-or-flight system, which, as its name suggests, prepares the body to either attack or run.

Having this explanation alone often helps teenagers feel *much* better about the times when they become uncomfortably nervous. When I'm talking with adolescents in my care about anxiety-provoking experiences, I'll often say, "I know that the physical symptoms that come with getting anxious can feel really out of control, but they actually have an ancient logic to them. The cave dweller part of your brain can't tell the difference between a tiger and a chemistry test, so it jacks up your heart rate and speeds your breathing in order to deliver heavily oxygenated blood to your large muscle groups. Your brain is getting your body ready to fight or run, regardless of what you're actually facing."

Teenagers also need to know about the nervous system's *parasympathetic* network ("para" meaning side by side), which takes over when the threat subsides and works to quiet the activity of the sympathetic nervous system and return the body to its resting state. Any time anxiety spikes and then abates, we are feeling the sequential effects of the sympathetic and parasympathetic networks. Should you receive a work email with the subject line

SERIOUS PROBLEM, your sympathetic nervous system will likely activate. If, upon reading the email, you realize that the problem isn't serious at all, your parasympathetic network will eventually activate and calm your body down. But here's the issue: A teenager who feels overwhelmed by anxiety or any other form of emotional turbulence might not want to wait for the sympathetic system to lay off and the parasympathetic network to kick in. This is where controlled breathing becomes the go-to hack.

Breathing deliberately—that is to say, deeply and slowly—starts the engine of the parasympathetic network. What's the mechanism? Our best guess is that controlled breathing is quickly detected by a network of nerves on the surface of the lungs. These nerves are constantly monitoring how we're breathing—lest we start to suffocate—and feeding that information to our brain. Under threat, the brain tells the lungs to pick up speed. But when we deliberately override that instruction by inhaling slowly and deeply, the nerves on the lungs register the shift in our breathing as evidence of *safety*, because that's how we breathe when we're safe. The nerves send this fresh, reassuring dispatch to the brain, which sets in motion the calming action of the parasympathetic network.

As soon as teenagers understand *why* deliberate breathing works to contain anxiety or other forms of emotional distress, the rest is simple. Sit down at a computer with your teen and search "common breathing techniques." You'll find plenty that appeal to your teen and are easy to get started with. For adolescents who get worked up quickly or often, it's a great idea for them to rehearse controlled breathing during ordinary, calm times so that they can more easily slip into deliberate breathing when an emotional tide is getting too high.

## How to Give Advice to a Teenager

Sometimes a problem that is bothering a teenager lends itself to a solution. Your teen has emailed an important question to a teacher but hasn't heard back and is now fretting, or she can't find the jeans she wants to wear and seems to be at her wit's end. When we adults can see a surefire way to manage the issue, it's nearly impossible for us to resist the impulse to offer advice. On occasion, our teen will immediately welcome and appreciate our guidance. But not most of the time. Usually, our advice-giving attempts go more like this:

Upset Teen: "*Ugh!* Today we got assigned to groups for a big project in history and my group got stuck with this kid named Troy. He's a total know-it-all who will try to take over the project, but he won't actually do any work. No one wants him in the group and the project is worth a ton of points. I'm so pissed!"

Caring Adult: "Hmm . . . maybe you can talk with the rest of the group about how to deal with him."

Upset Teen: "What? No! You just don't get it."

What happened? With the advice so sane, so unthreatening, so helpful and easy to apply, why didn't that go better? Well, it was due to a common and understandable misstep: Faced with an agitated teenager, our Caring Adult *skipped right past every option in the expression playbook* and instead jumped right into trying to use sage guidance to bring the emotion under control. I don't doubt that talking with the group would bring the Troy problem down to a tolerable size. However, it's extremely difficult for most teenagers (or adults, for that matter) to be open to advice until they feel that they've been heard out. If a teenager *asks* for your guidance, by all means give it. But if a teen is venting, you will almost certainly need to listen, empathize, and perhaps offer an emotionally granular encapsulation—as in "I *bet* you're pissed! I think that anyone in your situation would feel irritated, and also concerned about how this might play out"—before suggesting a solution.

Okay, suppose you've followed the right path, earnestly and adeptly doing all of the above, and your teen is still feeling rotten. *Now* can you make a suggestion? Not so fast! There's another item on the checklist first: finding out if our teen actually wants our help. You can say, "Do you want me to think with you about this?" If your teen does, then the advice-giving door has now been opened. If your teen doesn't want your help, don't despair, and give yourself some credit. Your teen may have gotten all of the needed relief from your excellent support of her emotional expression. Plus, because you have made it clear that you are available to consult on the problem, she's now aware that you're standing by to provide more support as needed—upon request.

Imagining that our teen *has* opened the advice-giving door, are we *now* free to walk through it? No, not just yet! Because we might be able to do even better. If we really want to help adolescents become adept at addressing complex problems, we should capitalize on teachable moments. Rather than handing your teen a solution, try working together to break down the problem and sort its pieces into two categories: everything that *cannot* be changed, and everything that *can*. "I get it," you might say. "It's not that fun to do a project with an annoying group member. Let's start by figuring out what you might have to live with and where you might have some say." Our hypothetical Upset Teen probably can't change the fact that she's stuck in a group with Troy. But she might be able to play a role in how the work gets divided, how the group members hold one another accountable for their contributions, and how, if Troy does get bossy, she and the rest of the group can choose to respond.

From here, you and your teen can bring your shared attention to brainstorming solutions for the parts of the problem over which your teen has some control. Now, at last, feel free to give advice. For best results, offer your pearls of wisdom as tentative suggestions, not the final word. "About the accountability," you could ask, "would it work to set checkpoints along the way to show each other how you're coming along with your contributions to the project? Might that help the group keep Troy on track?" As for the parts of the problem in the "cannot be changed" category, the goal is to help teenagers accept them for what they are, so that they can move on and not get stuck on them. One way to do this, especially with busy teenagers, is to encourage them to think about the smartest use of energy: "It looks like you're stuck with Troy, so you might not want to spend too much time wishing things were different. Maybe save your strength for the aspects of the project you can control."

## Changing Feelings by Correcting Thinking

When COVID-19 struck and adolescent mental health needs spiked, I was fielding calls from friends across the country who were looking for advice on how to find a therapist for their suffering teens. In a few of these cases the problem the parent described to me was circumscribed enough that it felt appropriate for me to offer informal help. "It may take you months to find a therapist," I would say. "In the meantime, I'd be happy to have a few calls with your teen just to see if I can be useful. It's not therapy, and if it's not enough to improve things, I'll help you figure out the next steps."

And so, even as the pandemic waned, I found myself on the phone with seventeen-year-old Daniel, who, though he was the son of a good college friend of mine, I had never met in person. Ahead of our call, Daniel's mom explained to me that he had recently been elected to a leadership position within his Jewish youth group. As part of that role, he was planning to take a summer trip to Israel with other high school students from around the United States. "Daniel's always been a little socially anxious," she explained. "He says he wants to go on the trip, but he's getting really worried about connecting with the other kids who are going. He's gotten himself pretty wound up about it, and any reassurance I offer doesn't seem to help. It's bothering him enough that he said yes when I suggested he might talk with you. That's not something my kid would normally agree to, so . . . it's pretty bad."

In my phone call with Daniel, he was immediately forthcoming. Talking from hundreds of miles away to a trustworthy stranger he would probably never meet seemed to create just the opening he needed. Polite and well-spoken, he quickly got down to business, sharing with me that he wanted to be excited about the trip but that he felt "like my social skills have gone backwards in the pandemic." He went on to explain that he had always been a little awkward around new people but that he did have a few good longtime friends. Daniel also mentioned that he knew a couple of the kids who were going on the trip, and that they were, in his words, "nice enough." But they were also very good friends with each other, and Daniel wasn't sure he could count on them for company. "I'm just really worried," he said, "that I won't have anyone to hang out with."

"What will the housing arrangements be? Will you have a roommate?" I asked.

"We're assigned roommates when we get there, but after we've been in Jerusalem for a while, we'll be traveling around a bit and staying in different places. I think as the trip goes on, people get to request roommates. I'm also worried that no one will want to room with me."

I asked Daniel more about the size of the group, what they'd be doing on the trip, how many adults would be present, and what kind of support those adults would provide. After he filled me in on all that, I offered empathy for how anxiety-provoking it can be to walk into a new, uncertain group dynamic—especially with social skills that felt rusty from the pandemic. Like Daniel's mom, I found that empathizing with his fears did nothing to help him feel better, so it was time to try another approach. Given that his going on the trip was a done deal, I decided to try to help Daniel see the situation in a new light.

I based this effort on my knowledge that when people are having an anxious reaction that's out of proportion to the actual situation, their thinking is usually off track in two ways: They are *overestimating* how bad the situation really is and *underestimating* their ability to deal with it. To try to course-correct Daniel's thinking, I started by asking questions about his fear that he wouldn't have anyone to hang out with, which I suspected was a bigger possibility in his head than in reality.

"It sounds like there are a lot of kids going on this trip, and most of them for the same reasons you are," I began. "Out of that number, there will be *some* kids that you don't have much in common with, but don't you think you might connect with at least two or three, even if you don't turn out to be lifelong friends?"

"Yeah, probably. I'm hoping that it will be better than that. But that would be okay."

Next, I turned my attention to Daniel's sense of helplessness.

"If, somehow, you do end up having trouble finding a friend or two, could you ask the chaperones for help?"

"That would be really embarrassing," Daniel told me. "I know they're there to make sure that everyone is getting along okay, but I would feel like a whiny little kid asking them to find me a friend."

"I get it," I replied, sympathizing with his response.

"But we've had some online meetings where the organizers have been asking us to do icebreakers. I haven't said much in those meetings, but it's clear that there are a couple of kids who are really into movies like I am, so when I meet them in person I think that I could start there and see how it goes."

"That seems promising," I said in a hopeful tone.

Now that Daniel had adjusted his assessment of the situation from dire to workable, I wanted to see if I could help him think differently about the outcome he feared the most. I began carefully: "Okay, I know you're worried that you'll somehow end up all alone on this trip, and I don't think that will happen. But I do think that you'll feel better if we look directly at that possibility and figure out what you would do if it did."

"Um . . . okay," he responded, sounding apprehensive.

"So let's imagine the worst-case scenario," I proposed. "If you really ended up feeling very lonely on this trip, what would you do?"

"Honestly, that would suck—it would bother me that I went all that way just to wait for it to end so I could go home."

"Okay," I said. "That's reasonable. And what would you do if you became very upset about it?"

"I might talk with the adults on the trip, or call home when I was alone. Also, I'd probably just read a lot. There are some books I've been waiting to get to and I've already put them on my phone."

"So, it would be really disappointing, but you could get yourself through it?"

"Yeah, I could. I wouldn't want to, but I could."

When teenagers can't change an unwanted situation, they can sometimes change how they think about it. Adults may intuitively find themselves pushing teens to do this when we say "But think about all the fun stuff you'll get to do on your trip!" or "I bet you'll find *lots* of kids to hang out with" or "Remember how lucky you are even to get to go on an adventure like this!" While these efforts of ours are well-meaning, they are rarely well received. In fact, they usually cause our teens to double down on their position that the situation is every bit as bad as it seems. Why? Because we're overshooting. Instead of aiming to help our teens become *happy* about the situation, we'd be better off aiming to help them become *more realistic* about it. I made no attempt to convince Daniel that he wouldn't run into any social problems on the trip. Instead, I set my sights on helping him *more accurately estimate* how bad the problems might be and what he could do about them even if they cropped up at their worst.

It's not always easy for teenagers to accept that they will at times have to live with some emotional discomfort. Nor is it easy for *parents* of teenagers—myself very much included—to be at peace with our teens enduring emotional pain. But think of it this way: Teenagers who are afraid of unpleasant feelings tend to confine themselves to narrowly constrained paths, while those who can tolerate some unease and uncertainty have more freedom. Daniel, for example, was able to take his trip to Israel (where he ended up having an excellent time!) once he accepted that he might run into unwanted, but manageable, social challenges. To help teenagers accept moderate levels of discomfort, it can be useful to try the strategies I used with Daniel. We can gently push back on their assessment of just how bad a situation might be and help them realize that they can handle the emotional stress that is actually likely to arise.

Alternatively, or in addition, we can help teens increase their tolerance for emotional distress by encouraging the practice of mindful meditation. For teens who may otherwise feel at the mercy of their emotions, meditation can build the capacity to observe feelings dispassionately. Among anxious or depressed teenagers, research has found that learning to regard emotions with detachment—to adopt the perspective of *noticing* feelings rather than *enduring* them—brings significant relief. That said, it can be challenging to get teenagers on board with the idea of committing to a meditation practice. But even teens who aren't into mindfulness might get something out of this bite-sized reminder that changing how they're thinking can change how they're feeling: Imagine that your mind is a pond full of fish. The fish are your feelings. Aim to be the pond.

## Helping Teens Adopt a New Vantage Point

As I've mentioned, I'm deeply fond of teenagers, often finding myself in awe of their loyalty, compassion, idealism, and inventive humor. So what I say next is not a dig, just a developmental fact: Normally developing adolescents tend to be more egocentric than people at other times of life. There's a certain sense to this. A main task of adolescence is to become a free-standing, defined individual, so teens naturally need to put more-than-average focus on themselves. But it also means that teens can easily get caught up in their own concerns, sometimes losing sight of the bigger picture. This usually isn't a big issue, and regardless, it tends to resolve itself as young people grow through and past their teenage years. At times, however, teens become preoccupied with self-focused concerns in a way that aggravates their emotional discomfort. When that happens, research shows that helping teens step outside themselves and observe their situation from a third-person perspective can help in two ways: It reduces their overall distress, and it allows them to think more rationally about the challenges they face.

In a study along these lines, psychologists invited a group of college students into a research lab and then asked half to imagine a situation in which they were cheated on by a romantic partner and the other half to imagine a situation in which their best friend was cheated on. Next, the participants were instructed to envision what the aftermath of the romantic offense would be for them (if they were in the first group) or for their best friend (if they were in the second). Finally, the participants were asked questions designed to assess their ability to reason objectively about the situation, such as "How many different outcomes did you see?" and "How much did you consider the perspective of the other person involved in the conflict?" The researchers found that the participants who imagined the situation happening to their friend were able to think much more carefully and objectively about it than those who imagined it happening to themselves.

In my clinical practice, I'm most likely to try to help teenagers adopt a new vantage point when they seem to be spiraling—when they get caught in the vortex of an unhelpful and disconcerting line of reasoning about a problem they're facing. On more than one occasion, I've watched a teen become increasingly agitated as she says, for example, "I think I just bombed a math test. This is gonna destroy my grade, and I'm sure that it will hurt me for college. Ugh! I'm the dumbest person in the world!" I don't dispute her reasoning or point out its many flaws. Instead, I try to get her to look at it from outside herself. "Let me ask you this," I'll say. "If your best friend said to you what you just said to me, what would you say back to her?" With a nudge this small, teens can often adopt a rational perspective on what right before had been a painfully consuming personal crisis. "Oh! I'd tell her that she doesn't even know how she did," the teen might say, "and that she might have done better than she thinks. Or that maybe everyone messed up the test and the teacher will drop it. And even if she did do badly, she still has time to get back points in the class and it probably won't change where she ends up in college. Also, it's not that she's dumb—she's just in a really hard math class."

While teens can often lighten their emotional loads by describing a personal challenge from a third-person perspective, their new take doesn't always stick. At times, adolescents will offer an even-handed—even generous—reply to their hypothetical friend but then go right back to beating up on themselves. For this, I've got a ready follow-up question: "What ideas do you have for why you would be so much gentler with your friend about this than with yourself?" I never know what response I'll get, but I can always count on this question to help the teenagers in my care continue to observe themselves from a curious, detached perspective rather than getting trapped in their own head.

You can put this strategy to work in your own home the next time your teen seems to be sinking in self-focused psychological quicksand. Consider, for example, a seventh grader who feels mortified when a so-called friend shares an unflattering picture of her in a class-wide group chat. To the tween whose picture has been shared, there's a good chance that this will feel like a profound and preoccupying humiliation. And there's an equally good chance that any reassurance offered by adults will fall flat. But it might be helpful to ask something like "How would you think about the situation if it happened to your good friend Riley? Would you feel embarrassed for her, or mad at the person who did it?" Moving from a first- to third-person perspective on the exact same scenario might help the tween be able to see the situation from a vastly more reassuring point of view.

A useful variation on this theme is to see if teens can gain temporal distance from what's making them miserable. Research shows that asking people how they think they'll feel in ten years about a situation that feels stressful today immediately reduces psychological discomfort. "I know that this feels really awful right now," you might say to the same seventh grader, "but can you picture yourself in ten years when you're fresh out of college? What do you think Future You would have to say about what Current You is going through now?"

## As Parents, Managing Our Own Emotions

Like many high schoolers, my older daughter spent the fall of her senior year laboring under the weight of the college admissions process. She did a great job of methodically getting through all that had to be done, but I was still anxious about how her applications were coming along. I think I can say in all honesty that this was not because I was personally invested in where she was admitted. But I did find myself desperately wanting the outcome that I knew my daughter was hoping for because I knew it meant a lot to her. And so on a Saturday afternoon in October I was suddenly struck by what felt (at the time) like a pressing question about whether she'd fully described one of her important extra-curricular activities in her applications.

When the question occurred to me, my daughter was at her job, so I reached for my phone to text it to her. By some miracle, I paused before firing off my message. Standing in my kitchen, phone in hand, I thought about how such a text would land on her. The retail store where my daughter worked was usually very busy, but I knew that she'd have a chance to read my text in a lull between customers. And then what would she do? If she agreed that I had put my finger on a real issue, she'd be in no position to address it. If she felt my worry was unjustified, she might feel compelled to send me a text explaining as much when she would know that she was really supposed to be focusing on her job. And if my question raised a point that warranted a longer conversation (as in "I asked my college counselor, and she said to do it this way, but I've been worrying about it . . .") she'd now be stuck thinking about that instead of enjoying work, the place where she normally got a welcome break from the college admissions process.

Put simply, sending my daughter an impulsive text would not be doing her any favors. Rather, it would succeed only in temporarily relieving *my* anxiety by dumping it on *her*. This, to be sure, would not have been the least bit fair or productive. So, just like stuck-in-the-chorus Jada at the start of the previous chapter, I "pulled myself together" and kept my worried thinking to myself until my daughter got home from work. When she returned, I even waited until she'd had a chance to get herself a snack! Only then did I say "I had a thought about your applications—is now a good time?" A brief and understandable eye roll later, I finally got to bring up what had sparked my concern.

Both of my daughters will tell you that I don't always handle my emotions as well as I did on that particular Saturday. But I definitely try, because as a psychologist, I know that managing my own ups and downs effectively is one of the most powerful ways to help my daughters handle theirs. Indeed, the topic of how emotion regulation among parents shapes emotion regulation in their children has been studied extensively, yielding a number of important findings.

First, our children learn a lot about how to navigate challenging emotions simply by watching how we do so. A parent who complains about a terrible day at work while pouring herself a big glass of wine is broadcasting one message about how to handle stress; the parent who says "Today was rough—I could really use some fresh air. Who's up for a walk?" is broadcasting another. Pushing Send on that message to my daughter would have suggested that thoughtlessly shooting off emotionally charged texts is an acceptable anxiety management strategy. Keeping that issue on hold until she got home communicated my sensitivity to what does, and does not, constitute an emergency. And asking her permission to raise the stressful topic of college applications demonstrated my ability to keep my daughter's feelings in mind as I sought to ease a worry of my own. If we want our teenagers to learn to manage their emotions well and to be circumspect about how their feelings might affect others, we need to make the most of our constant opportunities to show them what that looks like.

Second, how parents manage their own distress strongly influences the psychological climate at home, which, unsurprisingly, shapes the emotional lives of teenagers. Parents who tend to be highly reactive—to have strong, knee-jerk responses when they become stirred up—are more likely to have children who readily become anxious. Similarly, parents who display a lot of negative emotion, such as often feeling upset or angry, are more likely to have teenagers who suffer from depression, anxiety, or behavioral problems. This is not to say that parents should be feelingless robots—that's neither possible nor desirable. It is to say that if you or another adult in your home routinely struggles to find adaptive ways to express or control emotional discomfort, it's important to seek professional help for your own sake *and* for the sake of your teenager.

Finally, being able to stay calm when responding to unsettled teens goes a long way toward helping them regain emotional control. But of course this is not always easy to do. There's no question in my mind that, at least from time to time, *all* parents of adolescents react with anger to snarkiness, grow visibly anxious in the presence of an emotional meltdown, or become obviously sad when their teen runs into a painful disappointment. It is not necessary or even helpful for us to remain thoroughly unruffled by everything our teenagers bring our way—if our teen reports that on his way home he got a ticket for speeding in a school zone, it's perfectly fine for him to grasp from the tone of our voice and the look on our face just how unhappy we are with his poor judgment. That said, we should do our best to make ourselves a secure base that adolescents can count on when they need to psychologically regroup. How do we do that? By accepting that emotional upheaval is a central feature of adolescence and then working from the plays drawn up in this chapter and the one before it to help teenagers effectively regulate their moods.

How much does this matter for adolescent psychological health? A lot. Research shows that being able to take an interest in your teen's emotional turmoil and respond to it supportively provides immediate psychological comfort and can also protect adolescents against more significant psychological concerns down the line.

As if it weren't challenging enough to be attentive to how we react to our teenagers' potent emotions, many parents find that having a teen in the house stirs up a lot of feelings about their own teenage years. At times, raising adolescents can, quite unexpectedly, poke at old psychological bruises. I think here of a friend of mine who, as an adolescent, struggled with being overweight and was constantly made to feel ashamed about her size by her parents. When her own teen daughter started gorging on sweets to manage uncomfortable feelings, my friend felt as if she was thrust into a harrowing psychological hall of mirrors. While able to empathize deeply with what her daughter was going through in terms of the emotional eating, my friend was unable even to approach the topic because she was so unnerved to see history repeating itself, worrying that she was somehow at fault. To make matters even worse, she was hit by a new and piercing sadness for her former adolescent self. Now in the role of the parent, she realized that she would never treat her own child the way her parents had treated her. All at once, my friend became painfully aware of how unkind their behavior had actually been.

Thankfully, she was able to work with an excellent therapist who helped her sort through her multilayered challenge. From that therapist, my friend received professional coaching on how to address her daughter's emotional eating habits, and she simultaneously used the therapy to process her new recognition of how harshly she'd been treated as a teenager. "It was a really difficult time," my friend explained to me as she looked back on it, "but I can honestly say that being able to help my daughter was in itself therapeutic for me. I feel proud of having turned my awareness of my parents' mistakes into a chance to do better by my girl."

If you're struggling with how your teen's here-and-now intersects with your there-and-then, don't hesitate to seek support from a friend, a partner, or a professional counselor. Raising adolescents is, no question, an emotional workout that exercises us to the core. But like any workout, it's one from which we can gain strength.

## Recognizing Harmful Emotional Control

Sometimes teenagers fall into unhealthy ways of bringing their emotions under control—strategies that provide immediate psychological relief but come with a fearsome price tag. At the top of the list, of course, is relying on substances to blunt unwanted feelings. Getting drunk or high is, without question, a fast and effective way to tamp down emotional distress, but the cost to physical health and ongoing normal development can be astronomical.

There are other, less dangerous ways that teens keep emotions at bay but that still come with an unacceptably high price. One very common example is overreliance on playing videogames, mindless scrolling, or binge-watching movies or television to dampen emotional pain. Where is the line between healthy, equilibrium-restoring distraction and too much of it? Diversions are healthy so long as they help teens accomplish what they need to—such as the boy whose short visit to YouTube made it possible for him to tackle his homework. But they are a problem when they get in the way of a teen's schoolwork, sleep, chores, or anything else that needs to be done.

We should also be concerned if a teen is using compulsive behaviors to bring unwanted emotions under control, a phenomenon often diagnosed as obsessive-compulsive disorder. A teen's anxiety may be spiked by an intrusive thought (obsession), such as the worry that her hands are covered in germs, prompting an overwhelming urge (compulsion) to engage in a behavior that temporarily lowers anxiety, such as vigorous hand washing. Compulsions can quickly become a problem because they *work*—they provide immediate, if short-lived, emotional relief—but the risk is that they sometimes grow into an unshakable and debilitating approach to managing psychological discomfort.

Compulsive behaviors are often tied to a specific anxiety (e.g., the fear of contamination that leads to compulsive hand washing), but we should also keep an eye out for compulsions that are used more generally to thwart distress. These could include emotional eating—habitually turning to food as a main source of comfort—or compulsive dieting or exercise.

There are also teenagers who control their emotions by actively, and constantly, suppressing them. As soon as feelings start to bubble up, they use mental force to shove them back down. Such teens often end up at arm's length from everyone else, because actively quashing emotions, as we'd expect, gets in the way of forming and maintaining meaningful relationships. And bottling up feelings can take a toll in other ways, too. It interferes with the ability to remember details of experiences related to the feelings being suppressed, drains mental energy, and can, over time, contribute to cardiovascular disease and lead to wear and tear on the body that can even shorten life span.

It's important to note, however, that some teens are extremely reserved at home but share themselves freely with friends or trusted adults outside the family. From the perspective of the parent, this is hardly ideal. We love our teens, want to feel connected to them, and wish to know at least some of what they are thinking and feeling. This book, after all, centers on the relationship between parent and teen, because usually no one is more interested or better positioned than parents to encourage healthy emotional expression in teens. From the perspective of the adolescent, however, sharing important feelings with caring peers or adults other than their parents can work. In the time I've been practicing, I've cared for a handful of adolescents who, for any number of reasons, shared nothing with their parents but were quite open elsewhere and as a result managed their emotions well. If your teen is unexpressive with you but expressive with others, you may want to try to figure out what accounts for the distance in your relationship, but you probably don't need to worry that your teen is suppressing all emotions.

When, however, teens actively cut themselves off from all feelings and relationships, or they rely on substances, or diversions that derail the tasks of normal development, or compulsive behaviors, or any other harmful measures to bring their emotions under control, adults should seek the guidance of a mental health professional. Above all, we want to ensure that our teenagers default to healthy ways to both express emotions and bring them back under control when necessary.

# Conclusion

■ ■ ■ ■ ■

In the end, what view should we take of adolescent emotion? Given how intense, difficult, and even alarming teenage feelings can be, it would be easy enough to picture our teens' emotions as erupting fires—ones that spark, blaze, and at times seem ready to burn the whole house down, best prevented altogether, or at least quickly doused. But instead of fire, what if we thought of our teens' feelings as a flowing river, one that suddenly surges in adolescence? When the emotional waters get too high, we adults may need to help teenagers find healthy outlets for what they are feeling, to support them in expressing what is happening inside. At other times, we may be called upon to prevent emotional floods, to help our teens shore themselves up as they work to keep rising feelings within their banks and regain a sense of control. For the most part, though, we can let their emotional river run while appreciating the richness it adds and the growth it nourishes.

While a strong current has its dangers, it can also be a tremendous source of power. Welcomed and harnessed, adolescent emotions can provide the very energy needed to turn our teenagers into the connected, capable, and compassionate people we want them to be.

Connected? Yes. Healthy, gratifying relationships require emotional awareness. Our teens' ability to build and maintain connections hinges on their capacity to tune in to their own feelings and share those feelings with others. Emotions also strengthen the bonds between adults and teenagers. When adolescents bring us their fears, disappointments, and frustrations and we respond with curiosity and empathy, we reinforce our connection with them and model what we want them to expect in all of their close relationships.

Capable? Again, yes. Adolescents who are adept at managing their feelings can put one steady foot in front of the other even amid emotional swirls. Rather than becoming derailed by strong or unwanted feelings, they can rely on them as vital sources of information and motivation. And our adolescents' most powerful feelings, when met unafraid, can prompt their most growth-giving actions. Anger may inspire them to stand up for what's right; anxiety may spur a needed course correction; and even guilt or regret—once accepted and reflected upon—may keep them from making the same mistake twice.

Compassionate? Huge yes. Teenagers who are alert to and comfortable with their own inner lives are the ones who stand to be most interested in and concerned for the emotional experiences of others. What's more, being able to turn toward and withstand even the most challenging emotions makes it possible for our teenagers to put their natural idealism into practice, reaching out and extending themselves to those who suffer or are in need.

Let's embrace the full emotional lives of our teenagers and help them do the same. By doing so, we ready them to head out into the world prepared to grow, to thrive, to care for themselves, and to care about others.

# Acknowledgments

■ ■ ■ ■ ■

I cannot overstate how grateful I am for the wonderful people who support me in the day-to-day—my husband, my daughters, my parents, my dear friends. Regarding this book, thanks must go first to my phenomenal agent, Gail Ross, who gently nudged me to organize my recent thinking into this project. Without her encouragement from the beginning and throughout, this book would not have come into existence.

It was a complete pleasure to work once again with my brilliant editor, Susanna Porter of Ballantine Books, and with the entire, extraordinary team at Penguin Random House. In addition to benefitting from Susanna's wise editorial guidance, this manuscript was also improved by feedback from a world-class collection of early readers: Tori Cordiano, Anne Curzan, Lisa Heffernan, Candace Maiden, Annie Murphy Paul, Davida Pines, Kathryn Purcell, Marisela Santiago, Jonathan Singer, Amy Weisser, and Charlie Yu. And I could not have contemplated writing this book without the research assistance of the irreplaceable Amanda Block.

For helping me hash out the thinking presented here, I am indebted to my clinical colleagues Beth Ames, Hyunjune Lee, Janet Kemp, and Laura Voith. More broadly, I want to express my gratitude and admiration for the researchers in psychology and its related fields upon whose work this book relies. I have aimed to credit explicitly every individual whose scholarship contributed to the arguments and practical guidance I offer; any omissions or errors in this regard are mine alone. While writing this book, I was buoyed by the friendship and moral support of Hetty Carraway, Ann Klotz, Alice Michael, Cara Natterson, Reena Ninan, Mary Laura Philpott, Denise Clark Pope, Jennie Wallace, and Roberta Zeff.

My deepest appreciation is reserved for the teenagers and parents who have shared personal and often painful aspects of their lives with me. It is not easy to be—or to raise—a teenager, and this has been especially true in recent years. I remain in constant awe of how earnest, honest, creative, decent, and inventive teenagers are in good times and bad. It is my hope, above all, that this book not only serves them, but does them justice as well.

# Notes

ix  "I take it that it is normal for an adolescent" Freud, A. (1958). "Adolescence." *Psychoanalytic Study of the Child* 13, 255–78, 275.

ix  "It is a deep comfort to children" Ginott, H. (1965/2003). *Between Parent
and Child.* New York: Three Rivers Press, 21.

## Introduction

xviii  Antidepressant medications have been available López-Muñoz, F., and
Alamo, C. (2009). "Monoaminergic neurotransmission: The history of
the discovery of antidepressants from 1950s until today." *Current
Pharmaceutical Design* 15(14), 1563–86.

xviii  In 1987 only 37 percent Olfson, M., Marcus, S. C., Druss, B., et al. (2002).
"National trends in the outpatient treatment of depression." *Journal of
the American Medical Association* 287(2), 203–209.

xviii  By 2015 that number had risen to 81 percent Marcus, S. C., and Olfson,
M. (2010). "National trends in the treatment of depression from 1998 to
2007." *Archives of General Psychiatry* 67(12), 1265–73.

      Hockenberry, J. M., Joski, P., Yarbrough, C., and Druss, B. G. (2019).
"Trends in treatment and spending for patients receiving outpatient
treatment of depression in the United States, 1998–2015." *JAMA Psychiatry*
76(8), 810–17.

 xix  the most prescribed drugs in adult outpatient visits Stagnitti, M. N.
(2004, December). "Top 10 outpatient prescription medicines ranked by
utilization and expenditures for the U.S. community population, 2002."
Statistical Brief #60. Rockville, Md.: Agency for Healthcare Research and

Quality. meps.ahrq.gov/mepsweb/data_files/publications/st60/stat60.
pdf.

Cherry, D. K., Woodwell, D. A., and Rechtsteiner, E. A. (2007). *National
Ambulatory Medical Care Survey: 2005 Summary. Advance Data From Vital and
Health Statistics, No. 387.* Hyattsville, Md.: National Center for Health
Statistics.

Middelton, K., Hing, E., Xu, J. (2007). *National Hospital Ambulatory
Medical Care Survey: 2005 Outpatient Department Summary. Advance Data
From Vital and Health Statistics, No. 389.* Hyattsville, Md.: National Center
for Health Statistics.

Lewis, S. (2019, Sept. 5). "The top 50 drugs prescribed in the United
States." Healthgrades. healthgrades.com/right-care/patient-advocate/the
-top-50-drugs-prescribed-in-the-united-states.

xix **referred to wellness as an "emerging" industry** Lohr, S. (2010, May 23).
"The wellness industry as an echo of the Internet in the 1990s." *New York
Times.* bits.blogs.nytimes.com/2010/05/23/the-wellness-industry-as-an
-echo-of-the-internet-in-the-1990s/.

xx **$131 billion of the global wellness economy** Global Wellness Institute
(2021, December). *The Global Wellness Economy: Looking Beyond COVID.* The
Global Wellness Institute. globalwellnessinstitute.org/wp-content
/uploads/2021/11/GWI-WE-Monitor-2021_final-digital.pdf.

Callaghan, S., Lösch, M., Pione, A., et al. (2021, April 8). "Feeling good:
The future of the $1.5 trillion wellness market." McKinsey & Company.
mckinsey.com/industries/consumer-packaged-goods/our-insights/feeling
-good-the-future-of-the-1-5-trillion-wellness-market.

xx **the $100 billion global entertainment industry** Rubin, R. (2020, March
11). "Global entertainment industry surpasses $100 billion for the first
time ever." *Variety.* variety.com/2020/film/news/global-entertainment
-industry-surpasses-100-billion-for-the-first-time-ever-1203529990/.

xx **Studies consistently demonstrate that meditation** See, e.g., Goyal, M.,
Singh. S., Sibinga, E.M.S., et al. (2014). "Meditation programs for
psychological stress and well-being: A systematic review and meta-
analysis." *Journal of the American Medical Association Internal Medicine* 174(3),
357–68.

Goldberg, S. B., Tucker, R. P., Greene, P. A., et al. (2018). "Mindfulness-
based interventions for psychiatric disorders: A systematic review and
meta-analysis." *Clinical Psychology Review* 59, 52–60.

Gonzalez, M., Pascoe, M. C., Yang, G., et al. (2021). "Yoga for depression
and anxiety symptoms in people with cancer: A systematic review and
meta-analysis." *Psycho-Oncology* 30(8), 1196–1208.

xxii **survey conducted by the American Psychological Association** American

Psychological Association (2018). *Stress in America: Generation Z.* Stress in America Survey. apa.org/news/press/releases/stress/2018/stress-gen-z.pdf.

xxii **more serious mental health concerns have also been on the rise** Centers for Disease Control and Prevention (2019). *Youth Risk Behavior Survey: Data summary and trends report 2009–2019.* Centers for Disease Control and Prevention. cdc.gov/healthyyouth/data/yrbs/yrbs_data _summary_and_trends.htm.

xxii **high school students reporting significant levels of anxiety** Parodi, K. B., Holt, M. K., Green, J. G., et al. (2021). "Time trends and disparities in anxiety among adolescents, 2012–2018." *Social Psychiatry and Psychiatric Epidemiology* 57, 127–37.

xxii **symptoms of depression and anxiety among teens doubled** Racine, N., McArthur, B. A., Cooke, J. E., et al. (2021). "Global prevalence of depressive and anxiety symptoms in children and adolescents during COVID-19: A meta-analysis." *JAMA Pediatrics* 175(11), 1142–50.

xxii **many started to have difficulty sleeping** C. S. Mott Children's Hospital, University of Michigan Health (2021). "How the pandemic has impacted teen mental health." *National Poll on Children's Health* 38(2). mottpoll.org /sites/default/files/documents/031521_MentalHealth.pdf.

xxii **Studies conducted by emergency medicine departments** Yard, E., Radhakrishnan, L., Ballesteros, M. F., et al. (2021). "Emergency department visits for suspected suicide attempts among persons aged 12–25 years before and during the COVID-19 pandemic—United States, January 2019—May 2021." *MMWR. Morbidity and Mortality Weekly Report* 70(24), 888–94.

xxii **suspect that girls may have felt the social isolation** J. Singer, Ph.D., personal communication, April 2022. It is also true that even prior to the pandemic, girls were more likely to attempt suicide than boys.

   See, e.g., Ivey-Stephenson, A. Z., Demissie, Z., Crosby, A. E., et al. (2020). "Suicidal ideation and behaviors among high school students— youth risk behavior survey, United States, 2019." *Morbidity and Mortality Weekly Report* 69(1), 47–55.

xxiii **Compared to white teenagers, Black, Asian American** Stinson, E. A., Sullivan, R. M., Peteet, B. J., et al. (2021). "Longitudinal impact of childhood adversity on early adolescent mental health during the COVID-19 pandemic in the ABCD study cohort: Does race or ethnicity moderate findings?" *Biological Psychiatry Global Open Science* 1(4), 324–35.

xxiii **overlaid with a great number of other national crises** U.S. Department of Health and Human Services (2021). "Protecting youth mental health: The U.S. surgeon general's advisory." hhs.gov/sites/default/files/surgeon -general-youth-mental-health-advisory.pdf.

## Chapter One

6  **Plato imagined reason as a charioteer** Plato, *Phaedrus,* 246b.

6  **Descartes, a champion of rationality** Descartes, R., Adam, C., and Tannery, P. (1964). *Oeuvres de Descartes* (vol. XI, 448). Paris: J. Vrin. Modified from Descartes, R., Cottingham, J., Stoothoff, R., and Murdoch, D. (1985). *The Philosophical Writings of Descartes* (vol. I, 385). Cambridge: Cambridge University Press.

6  **Hume, flipping Descartes's script** Hume, D. (1739). *A Treatise of Human Nature.* London: J. Noon. As published in Hume, D., and Selby-Bigge, L. A. (1896). *A Treatise of Human Nature* (book II, section III, 415). Oxford: Clarendon Press; Internet Archive. archive.org/details/treatiseof humannoohume_0.

6  **She's a fellow clinical psychologist** T. Tobias, Ph.D., personal communication, March 2013. Terry, who has a great sense of humor, also introduced me to the concept of the "uterine locator device"—a fictional structure that explains the common experience in homes with a female parent that Mom is the one who always seems to be able to find things.

6  **To examine how emotions influence reasoning** Blanchette, I., and Campbell, M. (2012). "Reasoning about highly emotional topics: Syllogistic reasoning in a group of war veterans." *Journal of Cognitive Psychology* 24(2), 157–64.

6  **Their emotional investment in war-related topics** In contrast, other research has found that feeling stirred up for reasons that *don't* connect to personal experience can actually get in the way of the ability to think rationally. For example, one study found that a random selection of research participants had a hard time with logic problems related to fatal accidents, but not with ones related to cats. Presumably, questions about fatal accidents (but not questions about cats) sparked distressing feelings that took up intellectual bandwidth and got in the way of problem solving. Viau-Wuesnel, C., Savary, M., and Blanchette, I. (2019). "Reasoning and concurrent timing: A study of the mechanisms underlying the effect of emotion on reasoning." *Cognition and Emotion* 33(5), 1020–30.

12  **Teenagers, far more than children or adults** Gardner, M., and Steinberg, L. (2005). "Peer influence on risk taking, risk preference, and risky decision making in adolescence and adulthood: An experimental study." *Developmental Psychology* 41(4), 625–35.

13  **rises with every additional agemate on board** Tefft, B. C., Williams, A. F., and Grabowski, J. G. (2013). "Teen driver risk in relation to age and number of passengers, United States, 2007-2010." *Traffic Injury Prevention* 14(3), 283–92.

13  **the teenage brain is unusually sensitive** Albert, D., and Steinberg, A.
    (2011). "Judgment and decision making in adolescence." *Journal of
    Research on Adolescence* 21(1), 211–24.

14  **Awareness among legislators** McCartt, A. T., and Teoh, E. R. (2015).
    "Tracking progress in teenage driver crash risk in the United States since
    the advent of graduated driver licensing programs." *Journal of Safety
    Research* 53, 1–9.

16  **reading compelling narratives of lived experiences** Mar, R., Oatley, K.,
    and Peterson, J. (2009). "Exploring the link between reading fiction and
    empathy: Ruling out individual differences and examining outcomes."
    *Communications* 34, 407–28.

16  **the ability to take another person's perspective** Freeman, L., and
    Guarisco, M. (2015). "The wonder of empathy: Using Palacio's novel to
    teach perspective taking." *ALAN Review* 43, 56–68.

16  **only when young people become emotionally engaged** Kotrla Topić, M.
    (2021). "Emotional engagement, but not transportation, leads to higher
    empathy after reading a fictional story, in more agreeable participants."
    *Primenjena Psihologija* 14(2), 211–27.

16  **This point was made eloquently** Eliot, G. (1883). "The natural history
    of German life: Riehl." In *The Works of George Eliot,* standard edition:
    *Essays* (188–236, pp. 192–93). Edinburgh: Blackwood. (Originally published
    1856.)

22  **participants who had been maltreated** Heim, C., Newport, J., Heit, S., et
    al. (2000). "Pituitary-adrenal and autonomic responses to stress in
    women after sexual and physical abuse in childhood." *JAMA* 284(5),
    592–97.

23  **Whether an individual is traumatized** Ozer, E. J., Best, S. R., Lipsey, T. L.,
    and Weiss, D. S. (2003). "Predictors of posttraumatic stress disorder and
    symptoms in adults: A meta-analysis." *Psychological Bulletin* 129(1), 52–73.

    Bomyea, J., Risbrough, V., and Lang, A. J. (2012). "A consideration of
    select pre-trauma factors as key vulnerabilities in PTSD." *Clinical
    Psychology Review* 32(7), 630–41.

28  **weeping typically gives way** Gračanin, A., Bylsma, L. M., and Vinger-
    hoets, A.J.J.M. (2014). "Is crying a self-soothing behavior?" *Frontiers in
    Psychology* 28(5), 502.

    Gračanin, A., Vingerhoets, A.J.J.M., Kardum, I., et al. (2015). "Why
    crying sometimes does and sometimes does not alleviate mood: A
    quasi-experimental study." *Motivation and Emotion* 39, 953–60.

28  **help combat emotional overload** Freud, A. (1937/1966). *The Ego and the
    Mechanisms of Defense.* Madison, Conn.: International Universities Press.

29  **rudimentary defense systems** Beebe, B. (2006). "Co-constructing

mother-infant distress in face-to-face interactions: Contributions of microanalysis." *Infant Observation* 9(2), 151–64.

29   **managing an unpleasant emotion** Sandler, J., and Freud, A. (1985). *The Analysis of Defense: The Ego and Mechanisms of Defense Revisited.* New York: International Universities Press.

33   **asking nonsuicidal teens about suicide** Gould, M. S., Marrocco, F. A., Kleinman, M., et al. (2005). "Evaluating iatrogenic risk of youth suicide screening programs: A randomized controlled trial." *JAMA* 293(13), 1635–43.

33   **the factors that put teens at higher risk** Carballo, J. J., Llorente, C., Kehrmann, L., et al. (2020). "Psychosocial risk factors for suicidality in children and adolescents." *European Child and Adolescent Psychiatry* 29, 759–76.

34   **the most dramatic upticks** Ramchand, R., Gordon, J. A., and Pearson, J. L. (2021). "Trends in suicide rates by race and ethnicity in the United States." *JAMA Network Open* 4(5), e2111563.

34   **research fast-tracked by a congressional emergency caucus** U.S. Department of Health and Human Services. (2020). *African American Youth Suicide: Report to Congress.* nimh.nih.gov/sites/default/files /documents/health/topics/suicide-prevention/african_american_youth _suicide-report_to_congress.pdf.

34   **more likely to have recently experienced a crisis** Sheftall, A. H., Vakil, F., Ruch, D. A., et al. (2021). "Black youth suicide: Investigation of current trends and precipitating circumstances." *Journal of the American Academy of Child and Adolescent Psychiatry.* doi.org/10.1016/j.jaac.2021.08.021.

35   **Some young people come of age** One systematic review found, for example, that experiences of racism increase suicide risk among racial and ethnic minority youth. Rudes, G., and Fantuzzi, C. (2022). "The association between racism and suicidality among young minority groups: A systematic review." *Journal of Transcultural Nursing* 33(2), 228–38.

Black youth may be less likely to report suicidal thoughts or behaviors for fear of a punitive response. Intense emotions, including disclosures of suicidal thoughts and behaviors, are more likely to be met with punitive responses in Black youth than white youth.

See, e.g., Alvarez, K., Polanco-Roman, L., Breslow, A. S., and Molock, S. (2022). "Structural racism and suicide prevention for ethnoracially minoritied youth: A conceptual framework and illustration across systems." *American Journal of Psychiatry* 179(6), 422–33.

## Chapter Two

38 **when it comes to managing emotional distress** Hampel, P., and Petermann, F. (2006). "Perceived stress, coping, and adjustment in adolescents." *Journal of Adolescent Health* 38(4), 409–15.

38 **females and males are vastly more alike** Hyde, J. S. (2005). "The gender similarities hypothesis." *American Psychologist* 60(6), 581–92.

38 **even though the "average boy" is more physically aggressive** See, e.g., Björkqvist, K. (2018). "Gender differences in aggression." *Current Opinion in Psychology* (19), 39–42.

40 **They may assume that their daughter** Thomassin, K., Bucsea, O., Chan, K. J., and Carter, E. (2019). "A thematic analysis of parents' gendered beliefs about emotion in middle childhood boys and girls." *Journal of Family Issues* 40(18), 2944–73.

40 **fussier, given to crying** Weinberg, M. K., Tronick, E. Z., Cohn, J. F., and Olson, K. L. (1999). "Gender differences in emotional expressivity and self-regulation during early infancy." *Developmental Psychology* 35(1), 175–88.

40 **They smile less** Dodd, D. K., Russell, B. L., and Jenkins, C. (1999). "Smiling in school yearbook photos: Gender differences from kindergarten to adulthood." *Psychological Record* (49), 543–54.

40 **boys' expressions of sadness and anxiety dropped** Chaplin, T. M., Cole, P. M., and Zahn-Waxler, C. (2005). "Parental socialization of emotion expression: Gender differences and relations to child adjustment." *Emotion* 5(1), 80–88.

40 **only two feelings that boys show more frequently** Chaplin, T. M., and Aldao, A. (2013). "Gender differences in emotion expression in children: A meta-analytic review." *Psychological Bulletin* 139(4), 735–65.

41 **Research shows that parents are more comfortable** Birnbaum, D. W., and Croll, W. L. (1984). "The etiology of children's stereotypes about sex differences in emotionality." *Sex Roles* 10(9/10), 677–91.

41 **parents are more likely to turn their attention elsewhere** Chaplin et al. (2005).

41 **encourage their sons to limit "unnecessary" crying** Eisenberg, N., Cumberland, A., and Spinrad, T. L. (1998). "Parental socialization of emotion." *Psychological Inquiry* 9(4) 241–73.

41 **when our daughters are sad or scared** Kliewer, W., Fearnow, M. D., and Miller, P. (1996). "Coping socialization in middle childhood: Tests of maternal and paternal influences." *Child Development* 67(5), 2339–57.

41 **parents are more likely to urge their sons** Ibid.

41 **to help their daughters feel better** See, e.g., Cassano, M., Perry-Parrish,

C., and Zeman, J. (2007). "Influence of gender on parental socialization of children's sadness regulation." *Social Development* 16(2), 210–31.

42 **teenage girls demonstrate more empathy** Van der Graaff, J., Branje, S., De Wied, M., et al. (2014). "Perspective taking and empathic concern in adolescence: Gender differences in developmental changes." *Developmental Psychology* 50(3), 881–88.

42 **Girls are better able to imagine other people's perspectives** McClure, E. B. (2000). "A meta-analytic review of sex differences in facial expression processing and their development in infants, children, and adolescents." *Psychological Bulletin* 126(3), 424–53.

42 **to go out of their way to be helpful** Van der Graaff, J., Carlo, G., Crocetti, E., et al. (2017). "Prosocial behavior in adolescence: Gender differences in development and links with empathy." *Journal of Youth and Adolescence* 47, 1086–99.

42 **there may be an evolutionary reason** Christov-Moore, L., Simpson, E. A., Coudé, G., et al. (2014). "Empathy: Gender effects in brain and behavior." *Neuroscience and Biobehavioral Reviews* 46, 604–27.

42 **more likely to bring our sons in line** Ferguson, T. J., and Eyre, H. L. (2000). "Engendering gender differences in shame and guilt: Stereotypes, socialization, and situational pressures." In A. H. Fischer (ed.), *Gender and Emotion Social Psychological Perspectives.* Cambridge: Cambridge University Press, 254–76.

43 **researchers found that the mothers in their study** Flannagan, D., and Baker-Ward, L. (1996). "Relations between mother-child discussions of children's preschool and kindergarten experiences." *Journal of Applied Developmental Psychology* 17(3), 423–37.

43 **maintaining their social position** Eliot, L. (2009). *Pink Brain, Blue Brain: How Small Gender Differences Grow into Troublesome Gaps—and What We Can Do About It.* New York: Houghton Mifflin Harcourt, 262.

43 **research support for this hypothesis** See, e.g., Kraus, M. W., Côte, S., and Keltner, D. (2010). "Social class, contextualism, and empathic accuracy." *Psychological Science* 21(11), 1716–23.

43 **better than men at detecting anger** Di Tella, M., Miti, F., Ardito, R., and Adenzato, M. (2020). "Social cognition and sex: Are men and women really different?" *Personality and Individual Differences* 162(1), 110045.

44 **engage in rough-and-tumble play** DiPietro, J. A. (1981). "Rough and tumble play: A function of gender." *Developmental Psychology* 17(1), 50–58.

44 **Males remain more physically aggressive** Archer, J. (2004). "Sex differences in aggression in real-world settings: A meta-analytic review." *Review of General Psychology* 8(4), 291–322.

44 **hitting their peak level right around age fifteen** Karriker-Jaffe, K. J., Foshee, V. A., Ennett, S. T., and Suchindran, C. (2009). "The development of aggression during adolescence: Sex differences in trajectories of physical and social aggression among youth in rural areas." *Journal of Abnormal Child Psychology* 36(8), 1227-36.

44 **no clear link between testosterone levels** Duke, S. A., Balzer, B.W.R., and Steinbeck, K. S. (2014). "Testosterone and its effects on human male adolescent mood and behavior: A systematic review." *Journal of Adolescent Health* 55(3), 315-22.

  Also of note is this longitudinal study that followed 82 adolescent males from ages 12-13 to ages 15-16 and found a "general absence of T [testosterone]/aggression relationships" both in concurrent measures and over time. Halpern, C. T., Udry, J. R., Campbell, B., and Suchindran, C. (1993). "Relationships between aggression and pubertal increases in testosterone: A panel analysis of adolescent males." *Social Biology* 40(1-2), 8-24.

44 **between teen boys' testosterone levels and risk taking** Vermeersch, H., T'Sjoen, G., Kaufman, J., and Vincke, J. (2008). "The role of testosterone in aggressive and non-aggressive risk-taking in adolescent boys." *Hormones and Behavior* 53(3), 463-71.

44 **boys are more physically active** Thomas, J. R., and Thomas, K. T. (1988). "Development of gender differences in physical activity." *Quest* 40(3), 219-29.

44 **Boys who are highly empathetic** Carlo, G., Raffaelli, M., Laible, D. J., and Meyer, K. A. (1999). "Why are girls less physically aggressive than boys? Personality and parenting mediators of physical aggression." *Sex Roles* 40(9/10), 711-29.

44 **Parents are more likely to actively discourage** Ibid.

45 **just as likely as their female classmates to be unkind** Card, N. A., Stucky, B. D., Sawalani, G. M., and Little, T. D. (2008). "Direct and indirect aggression during childhood and adolescence: A meta-analytic review of gender differences, intercorrelations, and relations to maladjustment." *Child Development* 79(5), 1185-1229.

47 **girls express more anger than teenage boys do** Chaplin, T. M., and Aldao, A. (2013). "Gender differences in emotional expression in children: A meta-analytic review." *Psychological Bulletin* 139(4), 735-65.

  Wong, T.K.Y., Konishi, C., and Zhao, K. (2018). "Anger and anger regulation among adolescents: A consideration of sex and age differences." *Canadian Journal of Behavioural Science* 50(1), 1-8.

47 **Girls also outmatch boys** Chaplin, T. M., and Aldao, A. (2013).

47 **more likely than boys and men to face negative consequences** Evers, C., Fischer, A. H., Mosquera, P.M.R., and Manstead, A.S.R. (2005). "Anger and social appraisal: A 'spicy' sex difference?" *Emotion* 5(3), 258–66.

48 **Black girls are more likely to be punished at school** Perry-Parrish, C., Webb, L., Zeman, J., et al. (2017). "Anger regulation and social acceptance in early adolescence: Associations with gender and ethnicity." *Journal of Early Adolescence* 37(4), 475–501.

Wun, C. (2018). "Angered: Black and non-Black girls of color at the intersections of violence and school discipline in the United States." *Race Ethnicity and Education* 21(4), 423-37.

49 **generally viewed as being less in need of protection** Epstein, R., Blake, J., and González, T. (2017). *Girlhood interrupted: The erasure of Black girls' childhood*. Georgetown University Law Center: Center on Poverty and Inequality.

49 **generally viewed as being less endowed with childlike innocence** Goff, P. A., Jackson, M. C., Di Leone, B.A.L., et al. (2014). "The essence of innocence: Consequences of dehumanizing black children." *Journal of Personality and Social Psychology* 106(4), 516-45.

49 **Black girls are widely perceived as more sexual** It's important to note that modern views of Black girls as hypersexual or lascivious can be tied to a long history of subjecting Black females to dehumanizing stereotypes around their sexuality. Scholars have traced that Black females were long characterized as lustful and seductive in order to justify their sexual exploitation at the hands of white men who owned them as slaves or employed them as domestic workers.

See also:

Crooks, N., King, B., and Tluczek, A. (2021). "Protecting young Black female sexuality." *Culture, Health and Sexuality* 22(8), 871–886.

Gadson, C. A., and Lewis, J. A. (2021). "Devalued, overdisciplined, and stereotyped: An exploration of gendered racial microaggressions among Black adolescent girls." *Journal of Counseling Psychology* 69(1), 14-26.

West, C. M. (2006). "Sexual violence in the lives of African American women: Risk, response, and resilience." *VAWnet, National Online Resource Center on Violence Against Domestic Violence*, October. vawnet.org.

Collins, P. H. (2004). *Black Sexual Politics: African Americans, Gender, and the New Racism*. New York: Routledge.

French, B. H. (2013). "More than jezebels and freaks: Exploring how Black girls navigate sexual coercion and sexual scripts." *Journal of African American Studies* 17, 35-50.

Stephens, D. P., and Phillips, L. D. (2003). "Freaks, gold diggers, divas, and dykes: The sociohistorical development of adolescent African American women's sexual scripts." *Sexuality and Culture* 7, 3–49.

Though not as thoroughly studied as the hypersexualized stereotyping of Black girls, some research points to the application of similar stereotypes to Latina girls.

See, e.g., Rolón-Dow, R. (2004). "Seduced by images: Identity and schooling in the lives of Puerto Rican girls." *Anthropology and Education Quarterly* 35(1), 8–29.

49 **more likely to be sexually harassed** Espelage, D. L., Hong, J. S., Rinehart, S., and Doshi, N. (2016). "Understanding types, locations, and perpetrators of peer-to-peer sexual harassment in US middle schools: A focus on sex, racial, and grade differences." *Children and Youth Services Review* 71, 174–83.

Axelrod, A., and Markow, D. (2001). *Hostile hallways: Bullying, teasing, and sexual harassment in school.* AAUW Educational Foundation. aauw.org/files /2013/02/hostile-hallways-bullying-teasing-and-sexual-harassment-in -school.pdf.

49 **their complaints about harassment tend to be ignored** Rahimi, R., and Liston, D. (2011). "Race, class, and emerging sexuality: Teacher perceptions and sexual harassment in schools." *Gender and Education* 23(7), 799–810.

Wilmot, J. M., Migliarini, V., and Annamma, S. A. (2021). "Policy as punishment and distraction: The double helix of racialized sexual harassment of black girls." *Educational Policy* 35(2), 347–67.

49 **feeling both physically and emotionally unsafe** Opara, I., Weser, V., Sands, B., et al. (2022). "Feeling invisible and unheard: A qualitative exploration of gendered-racist stereotypes influence on sexual decision-making and mistreatment of Black teen girls." *Youth and Society,* 1–20. doi.org/10.1177/0044118X221075051.

49 **the adults they are hoping will step in** Harris, J., and Kruger, A. C. (2020). "'We always tell them, but they don't do anything about it!' Middle school Black girls' experiences with sexual harassment at an urban middle school." *Urban Education,* 1–27. doi.org/10.1177 /0042085920959131.

49 **they are viewed by much of the world** Cooke, A. N., and Halberstadt, A. G. (2021). "Adultification, anger bias, and adults' different perceptions of Black and White children." *Cognition and Emotion* 35(7), 1416–22.

Black girls face the same "hostility bias," but it is one that has been found to be even more pronounced for young Black males. Halberstadt, A. G., Castro, V. L., Chu, Q., et al. (2018). "Preservice teachers' racialized emotion recognition, anger bias, and hostility attributions." *Contemporary Educational Psychology* 54, 125–38.

49  **a study that starkly demonstrated this point** Halberstadt et al. (2018).

50  **(which for Black boys is already likely to be higher)** Goff et al. (2014).

50  **increases the odds that Black boys** Cooke, A. N. and Halberstadt, A. G. (2021).

Eberhardt, J. L., Goff, P. A., Purdie, V. J., and Davies, P. G. (2004). "Seeing Black: Race, crime, and visual processing." *Journal of Personality and Social Psychology* 87(6), 876–93.

50  **they are overdisciplined at school** See, e.g., Kunesh, C. E., and Noltemeyer, A. (2019). "Understanding disciplinary disproportionality: Stereotypes shape pre-service teachers' beliefs about Black boys' behavior." *Urban Education* 54(4), 471–98.

50  **racial profiling** McGlynn-Wright, A., Crutchfield, R. D., Skinner, M. L., and Haggerty, K. P. (2022). "The usual, racialized, suspects: The consequence of police contacts with Black and white youth on adult arrest." *Social Problems* 69(2), 299–315.

50  **arrest, detention, prosecution** Children's Defense Fund. (2011). *Portrait of inequality: Black children in America.* childrensdefense.org/wp-content /uploads/2018/08/portrait-of-inequality.pdf.

50  **lethal force** GBD 2019 Police Violence US Subnational Collaborators (2021). "Fatal police violence by race and state in the USA, 1980–2019: A network mega-regression." *The Lancet* 398, 1239–55.

Edwards, F., Lee, H., and Esposito, M. (2019). "Risk of being killed by police use of force in the United States by age, race-ethnicity, and sex." *PNAS* 116(34), 16793–98.

50  **endure the stomach-turning rite of passage** Anderson, R. E., Ahn, L. H., Brooks, J. R., et al. (2022). " 'The Talk' tells the story: A qualitative investigation of parents' racial socialization competency with Black adolescents." *Journal of Adolescent Research.* doi.org/10.1177/0743558 4221076067.

50  **It centers on advising young people** Ibid.

51  **We allow girls to express sadness and fear** Eisenberg, N., Cumberland, A., and Spinrad, T. L. (1998). "Parental socialization of emotion." *Psychological Inquiry* 9(4), 241–73.

51  **Boys are far more likely than girls to be diagnosed with** *externalizing disorders* Martel, M. M. (2013). "Sexual selection and sex differences in the prevalence of childhood externalizing and adolescent internalizing disorders." *Psychological Bulletin* 139(6), 1221–59.

52  **turning an unacceptable emotion** *back against the self* Freud, A. (1936).

*The Ego and the Mechanisms of Defense.* New York: International Universities Press.

54 **six times more likely to be suspended** Onyeka-Crawford, A., Patrick, K., and Chaudhry, N. (2017). "Let her learn: Stopping school pushout for girls of color." Washington, D.C.: National Women's Law Center.

55 **an approach that worked well** To ensure student safety, we also adjusted the settings so that no questions could be asked anonymously. I arranged with each school that I would follow up with the school counselor, if needed, to share the name of any student who asked about something particularly worrisome.

56 **Some guys feel comfortable expressing worry** Way, N. (2013). "Boys' friendships during adolescence: Intimacy, desire, and loss." *Journal of Research on Adolescence* 23(2), 201–13.

56 **they yearn for emotional connection** Smiler, A. P. (2008). "'I wanted to get to know her better': Adolescent boys' dating motives, masculinity ideology, and sexual behavior." *Journal of Adolescence* 31(1), 17–32.

57 **One research study found that Latino boys** Way, N., Cressen, J., Bodian, S., et al. (2014). "'It might be nice to be a girl . . . then you wouldn't have to be emotionless': Boys' resistance to norms of masculinity during adolescence." *Psychology of Men and Masculinity* 15(3), 241–52.

57 **mothers are more likely than fathers** Aznar, A., and Tenenbaum, H. R. (2020). "Gender comparisons in mother-child emotion talk: A meta-analysis." *Sex Roles* 82(3-4), 155–62.

57 **when they bring a personal problem to their dad** Dino, G. A., Barnett, M. A., and Howard, J. A. (1984). "Children's expectations of sex differences in parents' response to sons and daughters encountering interpersonal problems." *Sex Roles* 11(7–8), 709–17.

59 **kids hang out mostly with same-sex friends** Lam, C. B., McHale, S. M., and Crouter, A. C. (2014). "Time with peers from middle childhood to late adolescence: Developmental course and adjustment correlates." *Child Development* 85(4), 1677–93.

59 **rumination, especially for girls** Jose, P. E., and Brown, I. (2008). "When does the gender difference in rumination begin? Gender and age differences in the use of rumination by adolescents." *Journal of Youth and Adolescence* 37, 180–92.

59 **our daughters are more likely to ruminate** Stone, L. B., Hankin, B. L., Gibb, B. E., and Abela, J.R.Z. (2011). "Co-rumination predicts the onset of depressive disorders during adolescence." *Journal of Abnormal Psychology* 120(3), 752–57.

59 **ruminative thinking has been found to contribute** Young, C. C., and

Dietrich, M. S. (2015). "Stressful life events, worry, and rumination predict depressive and anxiety symptoms in young adolescents." *Journal of Child and Adolescent Psychiatric Nursing* 28, 35–42.

60 **Studies of how adolescent boys connect** "Boys, bullying, and gender roles: How hegemonic masculinity shapes bullying behavior." *Gender Issues* 36, 295–318.

Oransky, M., and Marecek, J. (2009). "'I'm not going to be a girl': Masculinity and emotions in boys' friendships and peer groups." *Journal of Adolescent Research* 24(2), 216–41.

65 **our daughters hit puberty** MedlinePlus, National Library of Medicine. (2021). *Puberty*. medlineplus.gov/puberty.html.

65 **the average girl is taller** Centers for Disease Control and Prevention. (2010). *Growth Charts*. www.cdc.gov/growthcharts/.

65 **many girls can run as fast and jump as high** Thomas, J. R., and French, K. E. (1985). "Gender differences across age in motor performance: A meta-analysis." *Psychological Bulletin* 98(2), 260–82.

66 **Puberty also drives a growth spurt in brain development** Van der Graff, J., Carlo, G., Crocetti, E., Koot, H. M., et al. (2018). "Prosocial behavior in adolescence: Gender differences in development and links with empathy." *Journal of Youth and Adolescence* 47, 1086–99.

66 **Middle school girls get better grades** Duckworth, A. L., Shulman, E. P., Mastronarde, A. J., Patrick, S. D., et al. (2015). "Will not want: Self-control rather than motivation explains the female advantage in report card grades." *Learning and Individual Differences* 39, 13–23.

66 **allows them to think in increasingly sophisticated ways** Silberman, M. A., and Snarey, J. (1993). "Gender differences in moral development during early adolescence: The contribution of sex-related variations in maturation." *Current Psychology* 12, 163–71.

66 **will try to manage the situation by taking girls down** At the time of this writing, I could not find any research that directly assessed the influence of pubertal development within victim-harasser pairs on the frequency of sexual harassment in middle school. Research does, however, firmly establish that girls who are further along in their sexual development are more likely to be the victims of harassment.

See, e.g., Skoog, T., and Özdemir, S. B. (2016). "Explaining why early-maturing girls are more exposed to sexual harassment in early adolescence." *Journal of Early Adolescence* 36(4), 490–509.

Goldstein, S. E., Malanchuk, O., Davis-Kean, P. E., and Eccles, J. S. (2007). "Risk factors of sexual harassment by peers: A longitudinal investigation of African American and European American adolescents." *Journal of Research on Adolescence* 17(2), 285–300.

One study that looked at harassers' pubertal levels does show that, in grade seven alone, boys' pubertal development is positively correlated with increased levels of cross-sex sexual harassment. Pepler, D. J., Craig, W. M., Connolly, J. A., et al. (2006). "A developmental perspective on bullying." *Aggressive Behavior* (32), 376–84.

Another study found that "pubertal status and the gender composition of the peer network were independently associated with increased likelihood of perpetrating cross-gender harassment, after controlling for age and gender" but, again, was not so specific as to assess the pubertal status of victim-harasser pairs. McMaster, L. E., Connolly, J., Pepler, D., and Craig, W. M. (2002). "Peer to peer sexual harassment in early adolescence: A developmental perspective." *Development and Psychopathology* (14), 91–105.

Which is to say that, as far as I could discover, the link between victims' and perpetrators' pubertal status has not been explored in the empirical literature, and thus I am basing my argument on height and strength averages and rates of sexual harassment by grade level. I have not, to my surprise, found evidence that this same argument has been made elsewhere. The most similar observation I found comes from Skoog and Özdemir (2016): "This, then, is an explanation that concerns girls' appearance and others' reactions to it; having a physically mature appearance in early adolescence, when one's peers still have childlike appearances, may underlie the link between early puberty and sexual harassment in early adolescent girls" (p. 493). If I have failed to credit any work that develops the same argument I'm presenting here, the error is entirely my own.

66 **boys are the ones more likely to tease** Gruber, J. E., and Fineran, S. (2007). "The impact of bullying and sexual harassment on middle and high school girls. *Violence Against Women* 13(2), 627–43.

66 **By seventh grade, if not sooner** Pelligrini, A. D. (2001). "A longitudinal study of heterosexual relationships, aggression, and sexual harassment during the transition from primary school through middle school." *Journal of Applied Developmental Psychology* 22(2), 119–33.

66 **often by making vulgar jokes** Hill, C., and Kearl, H. (2011). "Crossing the line: Sexual harassment at school." American Association of University Women. aauw.org/app/uploads/2020/03/Crossing-the-Line-Sexual -Harassment-at-School.pdf.

66 **by physically grabbing female classmates** Gruber, J. E., and Fineran, S. (2007).

66 **research shows that when boys bully girls** Rodkin, P. C., and Berger, C. (2008). "Who bullies whom? Social status asymmetries by victim gender." *International Journal of Behavioral Development* 32(6), 473–85.

67  **as a result of being sexually harassed** Ormerod, A. J., Collinsworth, L.,
    and Perry, L. A. (2008). "Critical climate: Relations among sexual
    harassment, climate, and outcomes for high school girls and boys."
    *Psychology of Women Quarterly* 32(2), 113–25.

67  **well-documented drop-off in self-esteem** See, e.g., Kling, K. C., Hyde,
    J. S., Showers, C. J., and Buswell, B. N. (1999). "Gender differences in
    self-esteem: A meta-analysis." *Psychological Bulletin* 132(1), 33–72.

70  **often referred to as** *gender-expansive* At the time of this writing, the term
    "gender-expansive" encompasses those who identify as transgender,
    gender nonbinary, gender-fluid, and genderless. PFLAG (2021). *National
    Glossary of Terms.* pflag.org/glossary.

70  **they have higher rates of substance use** Warner, A., Dorsen, C., Dunn
    Navarra, A., and Cohen, S. (2021). "An integrative review of experiences
    parenting transgender and gender diverse children." *Journal of Family
    Nursing* 27(4), 304–26.

72  **may also need to reconcile their love for their child** Abreau, R. L.,
    Rosenkrantz, D. E., Ryser-Oatman, J. T., Rostosky, S. S., et al. (2019).
    "Parental reactions to transgender and gender diverse children: A
    literature review." *Journal of GLBT Family Studies* 15(5), 1–25.

73  **teenagers who feel that their parents support** Hale, A. E., Chertow, S. Y.,
    Weng, Y., Tabuenca, A., et al. (2021). "Perceptions of support among
    transgender and gender-expansive adolescents and their parents." *Journal
    of Adolescent Health* 68(6), 1075–81.

    Pariseau, E. M., Chevalier, L., Long, K. A., Clapham, R., Edwards-
    Leeper, L., and Tishelman, A. C. (2019). "The relationship between family
    acceptance-rejection and transgender youth psychosocial functioning."
    *Clinical Practice in Pediatric Psychology* 7(3), 267–77.

## Chapter Three

76  **brain is starting to undergo a major physiological renovation** Arain,
    M., Haque, M., Johal, L., Mathur, P., et al. (2013). "Maturation of the
    adolescent brain." *Neuropsychiatric Disease and Treatment* 9, 449–61.

77  **somewhere around age nineteen** World Health Organization. (2014).
    *Adolescence: A period needing special attention.* apps.who.int/adolescent
    /second-decade/section2/page1/recognizing-adolescence.html.

77  **the neurological changes that begin during adolescence** Sawyer, S. M.,
    Azzopardi, P. S., Wickremarathne, D., and Patton, G. C. (2018). "The age
    of adolescence." *The Lancet Child and Adolescent Health* 2(3), 223–28.

    Arain et al. (2013).

77  **teenagers form them at a rate four to five times** He, J., and Crews, F. T. (2007). "Neurogenesis decreases during brain maturation from adolescence to adulthood." *Pharmacology Biochemistry and Behavior* 86(2), 327–33.

77  **it's also subtracting underused ones** De Graaf-Peters, V. B., and Hadders-Algra, M. (2006). "Ontogeny of the human central nervous system: What is happening when?" *Early Human Development* 82(4), 257–66.

77  **also speeds the transmission of the electrical impulses** Spear, L. P. (2013). "Adolescent neurodevelopment." *Journal of Adolescent Health* 52(2), S7–13.

78  **renovation does not proceed evenly** Casey, B. J., Jones, R. M., Levita, L., Libby, V., et al. (2010). "The storm and stress of adolescence: Insights from human imaging and mouse genetics." *Developmental Psychobiology* 52(3), 225–35.

78  **this final phase of the transformation** Arain et al. (2013).

78  **"I can tell you from both the research"** Maciejewski, D. F., van Lier, P.A.C., Branje, S.J.T., Meeus, W.H.J, et al. (2015). "A 5-year longitudinal study on mood varibability across adolescence using daily diaries." *Child Development* 86(6), 1908–21.

   Larson, R. W., Moneta, G., Richards, M. H., and Wilson, S. (2002). "Continuity, stability, and change in daily emotional experience across adolescence." *Child Development* 73(4), 1151–65.

82  **that we psychologists refer to as** *separation-individuation* Meeus, W., Iedema, J., Maassen, G., and Engels, R. (2005). "Separation-individuation revisited: On the interplay of parent-adolescent relations, identity and emotional adjustment in adolescence." *Journal of Adolescence* 28(1), 89–106.

89  **learning to have healthy disagreements at home** Asen, E., and Fonagy, P. (2011). "Mentalization-based therapeutic interventions for families." *Journal of Family Therapy* 34(4), 347–70.

89  **the hallmark of a constructive conflict** Van Lissa, C. J., Hawk, S. T., Branje, S., Koot, H. M, and Meeus, W.H.J. (2016). "Common and unique association of adolescents' affective and cognitive empathy development with conflict behavior towards parents." *Journal of Adolescence* 47(1), 60–70.

89  **the capacity to infer what another person might be thinking** See, e.g., Eisenberg, N., Cumberland, A., Guthrie, I. K., Murphy, B. C., and Shepard, S. A. (2005). "Age changes in prosocial responding and moral reasoning in adolescence and early adulthood." *Journal of Research on Adolescence* 15(3), 235–60.

89  **The ability to stand mentally in someone else's shoes** Crone, E., and Dahl, R. (2012). "Understanding adolescence as a period of social-

affective engagement and goal flexibility." *Nature Reviews Neuroscience* 13, 636–50.

89 **perspective taking increases significantly around age thirteen** Van der Graaff, J., Branje, S., De Wied, M., et al. (2014).

91 **raising adolescents is even more emotionally demanding** Meier, A., Musick, K., Fischer, J., and Flood, S. (2018). "Mothers' and fathers' well-being in parenting across the arch of child development." *Journal of Marriage and Family* 80(4), 992–1004.

91 **drawn to novel and exciting experiences** Romer, D. (2010). "Adolescent risk taking, impulsivity, and brain development: Implications for prevention." *Developmental Psychobiology* 52(3), 263–76.

91 **especially enjoyable and alluring for teens** See, e.g., Wahlstrom, D., Collins, P., White, T., and Luciana, M. (2010). "Developmental changes in dopamine neurotransmission in adolescence: Behavioral implications and issues in assessment." *Brain and Cognition* 72(1), 146–59.

91 **teenagers can be all gas and no brakes** Reyna, V. F., and Rivers, S. E. (2008). "Current theories of risk and rational decision making." *Developmental Review* 28(1), 1–11.

  Steinberg, L. (2007). "Risk taking in adolescence: New perspectives from brain and behavioral science." *Current Directions in Psychological Science* 16(2), 55–59.

92 **Research comparing adolescents from around the world** World Health Organization. (2011). *Global Status Report on Alcohol and Health*. who.int /substance_abuse/publications/global_alcohol_report/msbgsruprofiles .pdf.

92 **Much of the variance comes down to local norms** Steinberg, L., Icenogle, G., Shulman, E. P., Breiner, K., et al. (2018). "Around the world, adolescence is a time of heightened sensation seeking and immature self-regulation." *Developmental Science* 21(2), e12532.

92 **will make a material difference for their safety** Laird, R. D., Pettit, G. S., Bates, J. E., and Dodge, K. A. (2003). "Parents' monitoring-relevant knowledge and adolescents' delinquent behavior: Evidence of correlated developmental changes and reciprocal influences." *Child Development* 74(3), 752–68.

92 **When parents assume their teens will misbehave** Jacobs, J. E., Chhin, C. S., and Shaver, K. (2005). "Longitudinal links between perceptions of adolescence and the social beliefs of adolescents: Are parents' stereotypes related to beliefs held about and by their children?" *Journal of Youth and Adolescence* 34, 61–72.

92 **parents who talk openly with their teens** Guilamo-Ramos, V., Jaccard, J., Dittus, P., and Bouris, A. M. (2006). "Parental expertise, trustworthiness,

and accessibility: Parent-adolescent communication and adolescent risk behavior." *Journal of Marriage and Family* 68(5), 1229–46.

92  **articulate and enforce reasonable guidelines** Gray, M. R., and Steinberg, L. (1999). "Unpacking authoritative parenting: Reassessing a multidimensional construct." *Journal of Marriage and Family* 61(3), 574–87.

92  **less likely to drive recklessly** Shope, J. T. (2006). "Influences on youthful driving behavior and their potential for guiding interventions to reduce crashes." *Injury Prevention* 12, i9–i14.

Whitaker, D. J., and Miller, K. (2000). "Parent-adolescent discussions about sex and condoms: Impact of peer influences of sexual risk behavior." *Journal of Adolescent Research* 15(2), 251–73.

Guilamo-Ramos, V., Jaccard, J., Turrisi, R., and Johansson, M. (2005). "Parental and school correlates of binge drinking among middle school students." *American Journal of Public Health* 95(5), 894–899.

Chaplin, T. M., Hansen, A., Simmons, J., Mayes, L. C., et al. (2014). "Parental–adolescent drug use discussions: physiological responses and associated outcomes." *Journal of Adolescent Health* 55(6), 730-735.

95  **the many alarming headlines** See, e.g., Twenge, J. M. (2017, September). "Have smartphones destroyed a generation?" *The Atlantic*. theatlantic.com /magazine/archive/2017/09/has-the-smartphone-destroyed-a-generation /534198/.

95  **and even congressional hearings** Subcommittee on Consumer Protection, Product Safety, and Data Security (2021). *Protecting Kids Online: Facebook, Instagram, and Mental Health Harms.* commerce.senate.gov/2021/9 /protecting-kids-online-facebook-instagram-and-mental-health-harms.

95  **a link between the rise of cellphone use** See, e.g., Sumner, S. A., Ferguson, B., Bason, B., Dink, J., et al. (2021). "Association of online risk factors with subsequent youth suicide-related behaviors in the US." *JAMA Network Open* 4(9), e2125860.

McCrae, N., Gettings, S., and Purssell, E. (2017). "Social media and depressive symptoms in childhood and adolescence: A systematic review." *Adolescent Research Review* 2, 315–30.

95  **other research fails to support this sweeping conclusion** See, e.g., Coyne, S. M., Rogers, A. A., Zurcher, J. D., Stockdale, L., and Booth, M. (2020). "Does time spent using social media impact mental health?: An eight year longitudinal study." *Computers in Human Behavior* 104, 1–9.

George, M. J., Jensen, M. R., Russell, M. A., Gassman-Pines, A., Copeland, W. E., Hoyle, R. H., and Odgers, C. L. (2020). "Young adolescents' digital technology use, perceived impairments, and well-being in a representative sample." *Journal of Pediatrics* 219, 180–87.

95  **some studies indicate that digital technology can actually contribute**

See, e.g., Yin, X.-Q., de Vries, D. A., Gentile, D. A., and Wang, J.-L. (2019). "Cultural background and measurement of usage moderate the association between social networking sites (SNSs) usage and mental health: A meta-analysis." *Social Science Computer Review* 37(5), 631–48.

96 **seem to boost adolescent well-being** Beyens, I., Pouwels, J. L., van Driel, I. I., Keijsers, L., and Valkenburg, P. M. (2020). "The effect of social media on well-being differs from adolescent to adolescent." *Scientific Reports* 10(1), 10763.

Liu, D., Baumeister, R., Yang, C., and Hu, D. (2019). "Digital communication media use and psychological well-being: A meta-analysis." *Journal of Computer-Mediated Communication* 24, 259–74.

97 **don't like to be jerked around by adults** Bryan, C. J., Yeager, D. S., Hinojosa, C. P., Chabot, A., et al. (2016). "Harnessing adolescent values to motivate healthier eating." *PNAS* 113(39), 10830–35.

98 **having technology in the bedroom overnight** Gamble, A. L., D'Rozario, A. L., Bartlett, D. J., Williams, S., et al. (2014). "Adolescent sleep patterns and night-time technology use: Results of the Australian Broadcasting Corporation's Big Sleep Survey." *PLoS ONE* 9(11): e111700.

Bruni, O., Sette, S., Fontanesi, L., Baiocco, R., Laghi, F., and Baumgartner, E. (2015). "Technology use and sleep quality in preadolescence and adolescence." *Journal of Clinical Sleep Medicine* 11(12), 1433–41.

99 **Online pornography is so accessible** Sabina, C., Wolak, J., and Finkelhor, D. (2008). "The natures and dynamics of Internet pornography exposure for youth." *Cyberpsychology and Behavior* 11(6), 691–93.

99 **much of it is raw, graphic** Sun, C., Bridges, A., Johnson, J. A., and Ezzell, M. B. (2016). "Pornography and the male sexual script: An analysis of consumption and sexual relations." *Archives of Sexual Behavior* 45(4), 983–84.

100 **can be undermined by watching porn** Ibid.

104 **most adolescents are *not* having casual sex** Centers for Disease Control and Prevention (2015). *Trends in the prevalence of sexual behaviors and HIV testing. National youth risk behavior survey: 1991–2015.* cdc.gov/healthyyouth/data/yrbs/pdf/trends/2019_sexual_trends_yrbs.pdf.

Centers for Disease Control and Prevention (2017). *Youth Risk Behavior Survey Data.* cdc.gov/healthyyouth/data/yrbs/pdf/2017/ss6708.pdf.

104 **in the context of a meaningful relationship** Weissbourd, R., Anderson, T. R., Cashin, A., and McIntyre, J. (2017). "The talk: How adults can promote young people's healthy relationships and prevent misogyny and sexual harassment." mcc.gse.harvard.edu/files/gse-mcc/files/mcc_the_talk_final.pdf.

106  **the biggest slice in most homes would be labeled school** Östberg, V.,
     Almquist, Y. B., Folkesson, L., Låftman, S. B., et al. (2015). "The complex-
     ity of stress in mid-adolescent girls and boys." *Child Indicators Research* 8,
     403–23.


## Chapter Four

113  **The term psychologists use** See, e.g., Campos, J. J., Frankel, C. B., and
     Camras, L. (2004). "On the nature of emotional regulation." *Child
     Development* 75(2), 377–94.
          Aldao, A., and Nolen-Hoeksema, S. (2012). "The influence of context
     on the implementation of adaptive emotion regulation strategies."
     *Behavior Research and Therapy* 50(7/8), 493–501.

115  **better not to be entirely alone** Kennedy-Moore, E., and Watson, J. C.
     (2001). "How and when does emotional expression help?" *Review of
     General Psychology* 5(3), 187–212.

115  **we can measure the benefits of verbalizing emotions** Torre, J. B., and
     Lieberman., M. D. (2018). "Putting feelings into words: Affect labeling as
     implicit emotion regulation." *Emotion Review* 10(2), 116–24.

115  **research participants looked at upsetting photographs** Matejka, M.,
     Kazzer, P., Seehausen, M., Bajbouj, M., et al. (2013). "Talking about
     emotion: Prosody and skin conductance indicate emotion regulation."
     *Frontiers in Psychology* 4, 260.

115  **Researchers again asked volunteers to view distressing pictures** Taylor,
     S. F., Phan, K. L., Decker, L. R., and Liberzon, I. (2003). "Subjective rating
     of emotionally salient stimuli modulates neural activity." *NeuroImage*
     18(3), 650–59.

119  **research showing that teens with empathetic parents** Manczak, E. M.,
     DeLongis, A., and Chen, E. (2016). "Does empathy have a cost? Diverging
     psychological and physiological effects within families." *Health Psychology*
     35(3), 211–18.
          Other studies of note regarding the power of empathy:
          Eisenberg, N., Fabes, R. A., Schaller, M., Carlo, G., and Miller, P. A.
     (1991). "The relations of parental characteristics and practices to
     children's vicarious emotional responding." *Child Development* 62(6),
     1393–1408.
          Feshbach, N. D. (1987) "Parental empathy and child adjustment/
     maladjustment." In Eisenberg, N., and Strayer, J., eds. *Empathy and Its
     Development.* Cambridge: Cambridge University Press, 271–91.

Field, T. (1994). "The effects of mother's physical and emotional unavailability on emotion regulation." *Monographs of the Society for Research in Child Development* (59), 208–27.

121  **being able to describe inner experiences with precision** Nook, E. C. (2021). "Emotion differentiation and youth mental health: Current understanding and open questions." *Frontiers in Psychology* (12). doi.org/10.3389/fpsyg.2021.700298.

Wilson-Mendenhall, C. D., and Dunne, J. D. (2021). "Cultivating emotional granularity." *Frontiers in Psychology* (12). doi.org/10.3389/fpsyg.2021.703658.

121  **a line describing Mrs. Bennet** Austen, J. (1813/2003). *Pride and Prejudice.* New York: Barnes & Noble Books, 7.

125  **there's the issue of processing speed** Conway, A.R.A., Cowan, N., Bunting, M. F., Therriault, D. J., and Minkoff, S.R.B. (2002). "A latent variable analysis of working memory capacity, short-term memory capacity, processing speed, and general fluid intelligence." *Intelligence* 30(2), 163–83.

130  **most adolescents like their parents** Hadiwijaya, H., Klimstra, T. A., Vermunt, J. K., Branje, S.J.T., and Meeus, W.H.J. (2017). "On the development of harmony, turbulence, and independence in parent-adolescent relationships: A five-wave longitudinal study." *Journal of Youth and Adolescence* 46, 1772–88.

131  **we see our kids less as they age** Laursen, B., and Collins, W. A. (2004). "Parent-child communication during adolescence." In A. L. Vangelisti, ed. *Handbook of Family Communication.* Mahwah, N.J.: Erlbaum, 333–48.

132  **the same way that securely attached toddlers keep track** Waters, E. (1995). "The attachment Q-set (Version 3.0)." *Monographs of the Society for Research in Child Development* 60(2/3), 234–46.

134  **they include six components** Lewicki, R. J., Polin, B., and Lount, R. B. (2016). "An exploration of the structure of effective apologies." *Negotiation and Conflict Management Research* 9(2), 177–96.

140  **they'll sometimes listen to a song that matches their mood** Saarikallio, S., and Erkkilä, J. (2007). "The role of music in adolescents' mood regulation." *Psychology of Music* 35(1), 88–109.

140  **Psychologists recruited a group of adolescents** Sharman, L., and Dingle, G. A. (2015). "Extreme metal music and anger processing." *Frontiers in Human Neuroscience* 9, 272.

141  **they hasten a sense of relief** Van den Tol, A.J.M. (2016). "The appeal of sad music: A brief overview of current directions in research on motivations for listening to sad music." *The Arts in Psychotherapy* 49, 44–49.

## Chapter Five

147  **a surge in the capacity for abstract thinking** Piaget, J. (1969). "The intellectual development of adolescents." In G. Caplan and S. Lebovici, eds. *Adolescence: Psychological Perspectives.* New York: Basic Books, 1969, 22–26.

147  **can bring with it some very unsettling existential concerns** See, e.g., Hacker, D. J. (1994). "An existential view of adolescence." *Journal of Early Adolescence* (14)3, 300–327.

150  **a tactic that they often turn to intuitively** See, e.g., Wante, L., Van Beveren, M., Theuwis, L., and Braet, C. (2018). "The effects of emotion regulation strategies on positive and negative affect in early adolescents." *Cognition and Emotion* 32(5), 988–1002.

Lennarz, H. K., Hollenstein, T., Lichtwarck-Aschoff, A., Kuntsche, E., and Granic, I. (2019). "Emotion regulation in action: Use, selection, and success of emotion regulation in adolescents' daily lives." *International Journal of Behavioral Development* 43(1), 1–11.

154  **locking in at length on a disconcerting feeling** Zoccola, P. M., Figureoa, W. S., Rabideau, E. M., et al. (2014). "Differential effects of poststressor rumination and distraction on cortisol and C-reactive protein." *Health Psychology* 33(12), 1606–09.

155  **soothing activities also count for more** Bailen, N. H., Green, L. M., and Thompson, R. J. (2018). "Understanding emotion in adolescents: A review of emotional frequency, intensity, instability, and clarity." *Emotion Review* 11(1), 63–73.

Spear (2013).

156  **play videogames** Olson, C. K. (2010). "Children's motivations for video game play in the context of normal development." *Review of General Psychology* 14(2), 180–87.

Here's an illuminating quote from this study (p. 182): "Emotions play a surprisingly large role in children's motivations for electronic game use, particularly for boys. In our youth survey, two thirds (62%) of boys and 44% of girls who played electronic games somewhat or strongly agreed that they sometimes used games to help them relax; substantial numbers also used games to cope with anger (45% of boys and 29% of girls). Forgetting problems and coping with loneliness were also cited as reasons for play."

156  **choose mood-*countering* music** Saarikallio and Erkkilä (2007).

160  **people who aren't sleeping soon find that they struggle** Gruber, R., and Cassoff, J. (2014). "The interplay between sleep and emotion regulation:

Conceptual framework empirical evidence and future directions." *Current Psychiatry Reports* 16, 500.

160  **after five nights in a row of sleeping ten hours** Baum, K. T., Desai, A., Field, J., Miller, L. E., et al. (2014). "Sleep restriction worsens mood and emotion regulation in adolescents." *Journal of Child Psychology and Psychiatry* 55(2), 180–90.

161  **has been found to improve sleep quality** Lang, C., Brand, S., Feldmeth, A. K., Holsboer-Trachsler, E., et al. (2013). "Increased self-reported and objectively assessed physical activity predict sleep quality among adolescents." *Physiology and Behavior* 120, 46–53.

161  **the eight to ten hours of sleep** Paruthi, S., Brooks, L. J., D'Ambrosio, C., Hall, W. A., et al. (2016). "Recommended amount of sleep for pediatric populations: A consensus statement of the American Academy of Sleep Medicine." *Journal of Clinical Sleep Medicine* 12(6), 785–86.

162  **professionals who do high-stress work** Nazish, N. (2019, May 30). "How to de-stress in 5 minutes or less, according to a Navy SEAL." *Forbes*. forbes.com/sites/nomanazish/2019/05/30/how-to-de-stress-in-5-minutes -or-less-according-to-a-navy-seal/?sh=6633b09f3046.

162  **try to tell a profoundly upset teenager** This headline from *The Onion* is hilarious precisely because it's spot-on: "Alerts. (2022, March 1). Man would honestly rather keep having panic attack than do some stupid little counting bullshit." *The Onion*. theonion.com/man-would-honestly -rather-keep-having-panic-attack-than-1848563324.

164  **controlled breathing is quickly detected by a network of nerves** Streeter, C. C., Gerbarg, P. L., Saper, R. B., et al. (2012). "Effects of yoga on the autonomic nervous system, gamma-aminobutyric-acid, and allostasis in epilepsy, depression, and post-traumatic stress disorder." *Medical Hypotheses* 78(5), 571–79.

166  **try working together to break down the problem** This wisdom comes from Dr. Bruce Compas, a psychologist I interviewed for this article: Damour, L. (2017, February 8). "When a teenager's coping mechanism is SpongeBob." *New York Times*. nytimes.com/2017/02/08/well/family/when -a-teenagers-coping-mechanism-is-spongebob.html.

170  **they can sometimes change how they think about it** Troy, A. S., Shallcross, A. J., and Mauss, I. B. (2013). "A person-by-situation approach to emotion regulation: Cognitive reappraisal can either help or hurt, depending on the context." *Psychological Science* 24, 2505–14.

171  **learning to regard emotions with detachment** Yu, M., Zhou, H., Xu, H., and Zhou, H. (2021). "Chinese adolescents' mindfulness and internalizing symptoms: The mediating role of rumination and acceptance." *Journal of Affective Disorders* 280(A), 97–104.

172 **Imagine that your mind is a pond full of fish** Cosmic Kids: Zen Den (2019). *Be the pond: Mindfulness for kids.* cosmickids.com/video/be-the -pond-zen-den.

172 **adolescents tend to be more egocentric** Schwartz, P., Maynard, A. M., and Uzelac, S. M. (2008). "Adolescent egocentrism: A contemporary view." *Adolescence* 43(171), 441–48.

172 **It reduces their overall distress** Ayduk, O., and Kross, E. (2008). "Enhancing the pace of recovery: Self-distanced analysis of negative experiences reduces blood pressure reactivity." *Psychological Science* 19(3), 229–31.

172 **allows them to think more rationally** Kross, E., and Grossmann, I. (2011). "Boosting wisdom: Distance from self enhances wise reasoning, attitudes, and behavior." *Journal of Experimental Psychology: General* 141(1), 43–48.

172 **psychologists invited a group of college students** Grossmann, I., and Kross, E. (2014). "Exploring Solomon's paradox: Self-distancing eliminates the self-other asymmetry in wise reasoning about close relationships in younger and older adults." *Psychological Science* 25(8), 1571–80.

173 **the participants were asked questions designed** Ibid, 1573.

174 **asking people how they think they'll feel in ten years** Bruehlman-Senecal, E., and Ayduk, O. (2015). "This too shall pass: Temporal distance and the regulation of emotional distress." *Journal of Personality and Social Psychology* 108(2), 356–75.

176 **emotion regulation among parents** See, e.g., Bridgett, D. J., Burt, N. M., Edwards, E. S., and Deater-Deckard, K. (2015). "Intergenerational transmission of self-regulation: A multidisciplinary review and integrative conceptual framework." *Psychological Bulletin* 141(3), 602–54.

176 **learn a lot about how to navigate challenging emotions** Morris, A. S., Silk, J. S., Steinberg, L., et al. (2007). "The role of the family context in the development of emotion regulation." *Social Development* 16, 361–88.

177 **children who readily become anxious** Borelli, J. L., Rasumssen, H. F., St. John, H. K., et al. (2015). "Parental reactivity and the link between parent and child anxiety symptoms." *Journal of Child and Family Studies* 24(10), 3130–44.

177 **parents who display a lot of negative emotion** Stocker, C. M., Richmond, M. K., Rhoades, G. K., and Kiang, L. (2007). "Family emotional processes and adolescents' adjustment." *Social Development* 16(2), 310–25.

178 **being able to take an interest in your teen's emotional turmoil** Willemen, A. M., Schuengel, C., and Koot, H. M. (2009). "Physiological regulation of stress in referred adolescents: The role of the parent-adolescent relationship." *Journal of Child Psychology and Psychiatry* 50(4), 482–90.

180 **control their emotions by actively, and constantly, suppressing them**
The cost of emotional suppression turns out to be culturally specific.
Psychologists use the term *display rules* to describe the patterns of
emotional expression that are considered to be appropriate within a
particular social group. In the broadest strokes, collectivistic cultures are
more likely to mask intense emotions, while members of individualistic
cultures are more likely to express their emotions freely. For example,
one study found that when Europeans and European Americans were
asked to *suppress* feelings of anger, their heart rate and blood pressure
went up; in contrast, heart rate and blood pressure rose for Chinese when
they were instructed to *express* angry feelings. Zhou, T., and Bishop, G. D.
(2021). "Culture moderates the cardiovascular consequence of anger
regulation strategy." *International Journal of Psychophysiology* 8(3), 291–98.
See also:
Butler, E. A., Lee, T. L., and Gross, J. J. (2007). "Emotion regulation and
culture: Are the social consequences of emotion suppression culture-
specific?" *Emotion* 7(1), 30–48.
Matsumoto, D., Willingham, B., and Olide, A. (2009). "Sequential
dynamics of culturally moderated facial expressions." *Psychological Science*
20(10), 1269–74.

180 **gets in the way of forming and maintaining meaningful relationships**
Butler, E. A., Egloff, B., Wilhelm, F. H., et al. (2003). "The social consequences of expressive suppression." *Emotion* 3(1), 48–67.

180 **interferes with the ability to remember details** Richards, J. M., and
Gross, J. J. (1999). "Composure at any cost? The cognitive consequences
of emotion suppression." *Personality and Social Psychology Bulletin* 25(8),
1033–44.

180 **drains mental energy** Baumeister, R. F., Bratslavsky, E., Muraven, M., and
Tice, D. M. (1998). "Ego depletion: Is the active self a limited resource?"
*Journal of Personality and Social Psychology* 74(5), 1252–65.

180 **contribute to cardiovascular disease** Quartana, P. J., and Burns, J. W.
(2010). "Emotion suppression affects cardiovascular responses to initial
and subsequent laboratory stressors." *British Journal of Health Psychology*
15(3), 511–28.

180 **can even shorten life span** Chapman, B. P, Fiscella, K., Kawachi, I., et al.
(2013). "Emotion suppression and mortality risk over a 12-year follow-
up." *Journal of Psychosomatic Research* 75(4), 381–85.

# Recommended Resources

■ ▪ ■ ▪ ■

## Adolescent Development

Duffy, J. (2019). *Parenting the New Teen in the Age of Anxiety: A Complete Guide to Your Child's Stressed, Depressed, Expanded, Amazing Adolescence.* Miami: Mango Publishing.

Heffernan, L., and Harrington, M. (2019). *Grown and Flown: How to Support Your Teen, Stay Close as a Family, and Raise Independent Adults.* New York: Flatiron Books.

Icard, M. (2020). *Fourteen Talks by Age Fourteen: The Essential Conversations You Need to Have With Your Kids Before They Start High School.* New York: Harmony Books.

Jensen, F. E. (2016). *The Teenage Brain: A Neuroscientist's Survival Guide to Raising Adolescents and Young Adults.* New York: Harper.

Lythcott-Haims, J. (2015). *How to Raise an Adult: Break Free of the Overparenting Trap and Prepare Your Kid for Success.* New York: St. Martin's Press.

Siegel, D. J. (2014). *Brainstorm: The Power and Purpose of the Teenage Brain.* New York: TarcherPerigee.

Steinberg, L. (2015). *Age of Opportunity: Lessons from the New Science of Adolescence.* New York: Harper.

## Emotion

Barrett, L. F. (2017). *How Emotions Are Made: The Secret Life of the Brain.* New York: Mariner Books.

Brackett, M. (2019). *Permission to Feel: The Power of Emotional Intelligence to Achieve Well-Being and Success.* New York: Celadon Books.

Damasio, A. (1999). *The Feeling of What Happens: Body and Emotion in the Making of Consciousness.* New York: Harcourt.

Damour, L. (2019). *Under Pressure: Confronting the Epidemic of Stress and Anxiety in Girls.* New York: Ballantine Books.

Oatley, K., Keltner, D., and Jenkins, J. M. (2019). *Understanding Emotions,* fourth edition. Hoboken, N.J.: Wiley.

Van der Kolk, B. (2014). *The Body Keeps the Score: Brain, Mind, and Body in Healing.* New York: Penguin Books.

## Gender

Damour, L. (2016). *Untangled: Guiding Teenage Girls Through the Seven Transitions into Adulthood.* New York: Ballantine Books.

Natterson, C. (2020). *Decoding Boys: New Science Behind the Subtle Art of Raising Sons.* New York: Ballantine Books.

Eliot, L. (2010). *Pink Brain, Blue Brain: How Small Differences Grow into Troublesome Gaps—and What We Can Do About It.* New York: Mariner Books.

Kindlon, D., and Thompson, M. (1999). *Raising Cain: Protecting the Emotional Lives of Boys.* New York: Ballantine Books.

Pipher, M., and Gilliam, S. (2019). *Reviving Ophelia 25th Anniversary Edition: Saving the Selves of Adolescent Girls.* New York: Riverhead Books.

## Marginalized Adolescents

Belgrave, F. Z. (2009). *African American Girls: Reframing Perceptions and Changing Experiences.* New York: Springer.

Belgrave, F. Z., and Brevard, J. K. (2014). *African American Boys: Identity, Culture, and Development.* New York: Springer.

Crockett, L. J., and Carlo, G., eds. (2016). *Rural Ethnic Minority Youth and Families in the United States: Theory, Research, and Applications.* New York: Springer.

Forcier, M., Van Schalkwyk, G., and Turban, J. L., eds. (2020). *Pediatric Gender Identity: Gender-Affirming Care for Transgender and Gender Diverse Youth.* New York: Springer.

Golden, M. (2022). *Saving Our Sons: Raising Black Children in a Turbulent World.* Miami: Mango Publishing.

Morris, M. W. (2018). *Pushout: The Criminalization of Black Girls in Schools.* New York: The New Press.

Janssen, A., and Leibowitz, S., eds. (2018). *Affirmative Mental Health Care for Transgender and Gender Diverse Youth: A Clinical Guide.* New York: Springer.

Russell, S. T., Crockett, L. J., and Chao, R. K., eds. (2010). *Asian American Parenting and Parent-Adolescent Relationships*. New York: Springer.


## Books for Teenagers

Bacow, T. (2021). *Goodbye Anxiety: A Guided Journal for Overcoming Worry*. Seattle: Sasquatch Books.

Hurley, K. (2019). *The Depression Workbook for Teens: Tools to Improve Your Mood, Build Self-Esteem, and Stay Motivated*. Emeryville, Calif: Rockridge Press.

Knaus, W. J. (2016). *Overcoming Procrastination for Teens: A CBT Guide for College-Bound Students*. Oakland, Calif: Instant Help Books.

Schab, L. M. (2021). *The Anxiety Workbook for Teens: Activities to Help You Deal with Anxiety and Worry,* second edition. Oakland, Calif: Instant Help Books.

Sedley, B. (2017). *Stuff That Sucks: A Teen's Guide to Accepting What You Can't Change and Committing to What You Can*. Oakland, Calif: Instant Help Books.

Stahl, B., and Goldstein, E. (2010). *A Mindfulness-based Stress Reduction Workbook*. Oakland, Calif: New Harbinger.

# Index

■ ■ ■ ■ ■

PHOTO: © JEFF DOWNIE

Recognized as a thought leader by the American Psychological Association, LISA DAMOUR, PH.D., co-hosts the *Ask Lisa* podcast and works in collaboration with UNICEF. She also maintains a clinical practice and is a regular contributor to *The New York Times* and CBS News. Dr. Damour is the author of three *New York Times* bestsellers, *Untangled: Guiding Teenage Girls Through the Seven Transitions into Adulthood, Under Pressure: Confronting the Epidemic of Stress and Anxiety in Girls,* and *The Emotional Lives of Teenagers: Raising Connected, Capable, and Compassionate Adolescents.* She lives with her husband and two daughters in Shaker Heights, Ohio.

drlisadamour.com
Instagram: @lisa.damour
Facebook.com/lisadamourphd
Twitter: @LDamour
Podcast: @asklisapodcast

## About the Type

■ ▪ ■ ▪ ■

This book was set in Legacy, a typeface family designed by Ronald Arnholm (b. 1939) and issued in digital form by ITC in 1992. Both its serifed and unserifed versions are based on an original type created by the French punchcutter Nicholas Jenson in the late fifteenth century. While Legacy tends to differ from Jenson's original in its proportions, it maintains much of the latter's characteristic modulations in stroke.